25¢

Landmark

From
Alison
Baker

D1488286

HEROINES OF THE EARLY WEST

Heroines of the Early West

NANCY WILSON ROSS

ILLUSTRATED BY PAUL GALDONE

RANDOM HOUSE   NEW YORK

The material in this book first appeared, in somewhat different form, in *Westward
the Women* by Nancy Wilson Ross (1944).

CONTENTS

HEROINES OF THE EARLY WEST

CHAPTER ONE

OVER THE TOP OF THE WORLD

*T*HIS is a book about some amazing women who lived only a little over a hundred years ago in this country—a space of time which, you might say, is hardly even a blink of History's eye. Although these women were quite like your own mothers and aunts, they lived their lives in such a remarkable way that we now call them "heroines."

The chief and most important thing these women did was to make America the size and shape it is today. If these pioneers had not had the courage and the strength to travel thousands of miles across unknown land, on foot, on horseback, or in crude covered wagons, in order to set up primitive housekeeping among wild animals and savage Indians, the United States would not appear on a map as we now know it.

In the early and mid-part of the nineteenth century, eminent men in the young United States thought it nothing short of "insane" to want to explore and claim the Far West. Mr. Daniel Webster was just one of many famous statesmen who was convinced Americans should not even bother their heads about the vast unknown territory that lay beyond the Rocky Mountains. He rose in the United States Senate and made some remarks on the subject which now seem very funny indeed.

"What can we do with the Western coast," he inquired, "a coast of 3,000 miles, rockbound, cheerless, uninviting, and not a harbor on it?" (Since no one had seen this coast, there was no one to answer his question and only a visionary could have imagined the great harbor cities that now lie along the Pacific shoreline.) Mr. Webster went on in his best oratorical tones to demand, "What use have we for such a country? I will not vote one cent from the public treasury to place the Pacific Ocean one inch nearer Boston than it is now."

Mr. Webster was not alone in this negative point of view. A senator from South Carolina said he personally wouldn't "give a pinch of snuff for the whole western territory." Another gentleman was of the opinion that it was Providence herself who had set the great western mountains as an "impassable natural boundary," to show Americans they were intended to remain well to the east of the Rockies.

But, oddly enough, in spite of these pronouncements from the very wisest people a strange thing began to happen. At first slowly and quietly, like a small trickle of water from melting snow, and then with ever increasing force until it was a flood tide, Americans began to move westward.

It was not men alone who set out on this perilous venture to lands then as "foreign" and distant as Africa or India, but women too. Wives, sisters, daughters, even widows with their children, embarked courageously on the long, exhausting and dangerous western trek. Nothing could seem to hold the women back—not even terrifying stories about cannibal Indians, fever-ridden swamps, strange wild beasts, poisonous snakes, mountains too high to climb, rivers too deep to ford, forests that were trackless jungles.

And it was these plucky women "emigrants" from the East Coast and the Midwest who, in time, gave the United States its strongest claim to the vast stretch of western country which Great Britain had confidently expected to keep for herself. For the presence of white women in the farthest western wilderness was a new and vital factor. Women offered proof to the world that Americans were not traveling so far from civilization just to make quick fortunes in gold or furs. They had come west to establish homes and raise children. They called themselves "settlers."

What is more, even though these emigrants took up life in a "foreign" part of the continent, both men and women stubbornly continued to regard themselves as Americans. At last the government in Washington had to recognize their existence and say "Hands off" to other claimants of this part of the American land. And so the western boundary of the present United States became Mr. Webster's "rockbound, cheerless, uninviting" Pacific Coast—now generally considered, among other things, a "vacationer's paradise" from the southernmost tip of California to the Canadian border of the state of Washington.

It is fortunate for us who live today that there were women, and girls too, who somehow found the time and energy, as they crossed the "great dry sea" of the plains, climbed the "impassable natural barrier" of the western mountains, or settled in the "uninhabitable" wilderness, to keep diaries and write letters. Others, looking back as old ladies on their once "unimaginable" adventure, would tell stories to their descendants, and occasionally these descendants had the wisdom to write down what their mothers or their grandmothers had told them about episodes of the "old days." From these valuable records we have been able to learn a great deal about what life was like for a woman during the long months of the western push and the first years of hardship and loneliness on the farthest frontier.

These diarists, letter-writers and autobiographers of the Far West, in the years between the 1830s and the early 1900s, were, though perhaps unaware of it, serving History as ably as any trained historian. All modern historians must be eternally grateful for the urge that led these girls and women to write down their day-to-day experiences. Not every one was this wise, you may be sure. One old grandmother who had been asked a great many questions about crossing the plains and early pioneering exclaimed in surprise, "I didn't know

those common every-day things would ever be history!"

Some of the women diarists were highly intelligent, even "literary," like Narcissa Whitman and Abigail Scott Duniway. Some of them, like Mary Walker, were natural keepers of records. Washington State College has a faded letter to Mary's husband from the factor of a Hudson's Bay fort begging to know the birth dates of his own half-Indian sons who, about to be sent off to Europe to get an education, needed birth certificates. The factor himself had not made note of their birth dates—unbelievable as that may seem—nor had his Indian wife. But he remembered Mary Walker, when on a visit, jotting down the names and dates in her "pocket Book." Somehow Mary, who came from Maine, must have sensed the importance of these small details in a land still without town clerks or, for that matter, towns! The first "vital statistics" in Old Oregon are to be found in records kept by women: the minute book of the Columbia Maternal Association, founded in the year 1838 by some missionary wives who came west with their husbands to "Christianize" the Indians. These particular statistics are the lists of the Association's widely scattered members, the dates on which they joined, new members as they were taken in, the dates of their children's births and deaths, and the minutes of their infrequent meetings.

Sometimes these old discolored letters, journals and books tell us a lot. Sometimes they only hint about incidents that would be hair-raising today, although then they were taken very much in stride.

From the dozens of episodes in library and museum files and the tales of "old timers" come tantalizing fragments, scraps of exciting plot, hints of lively personalities that tease and haunt the mind.

It would be fun to know more, for instance, about a certain Mrs. David Blaine who was the spicy-tongued wife of the first minister in pioneer Seattle. During an Indian uprising she, having just given birth to her first child, was rowed out in an armchair to a gunboat that chanced to be in the harbor. In this same armchair she was hoisted aboard with her newborn babe in her arms. After a few days on the gunboat, when nothing seemed to be happening on shore, she insisted on being rowed back and forth several times to her abandoned log cabin, to have a look and to "wash and iron and do some other work." She apparently felt able to cope with any Indian she met. What is more, she took the baby with her.

Calmly and with humor Mrs. Blaine wrote a letter home to her distant family—a letter which still survives. "The babe is a month old today and I guess has been tossed about as much as a child of his age ever was. The ship is some distance from shore so that we have to go back and forth in a small boat. He has been taken ashore some half dozen times or more. . . . He stands it pretty well though he cries considerably from wind on his stomach, is as fat as a pig and dreadfully homely."

Obviously Mrs. Blaine knew nothing about fear —or if she did she had conquered it. Perhaps she had made up her mind not to give way to it when she set out on her western journey. Every woman and girl of those early days had to learn to live with constant danger. If they were going to be afraid there was certainly plenty to cause them fear. Wild animals. Indians. Sickness or injury— and no doctor at hand. Losing their way—for many wagon trains took fatal "short cuts" and lost their bearings. Sudden death—and no one to bury the dead or lend a helping hand. Storms, and no shelter from rain, snow, hail or lightning. Hunger. Loneliness. Above all, just fear of the "great unknown," that mysterious force that breathed in the untrod forests, beat in the tide of unexplored waterways, lurked around the bends of wild rivers or rugged shorelines, rang in the nighttime bark of wolf or coyote, shimmered in the heat haze of an endless prairie, danced in the dervish dance of bunch grass over the dry desert.

Already on the trip west, even before they had reached the country where hostile Indians lived and where the land was rough and unfriendly, there were many possible perils. On that long trek west high-strung women often "wore themselves to a frazzle" with the necessity for constant watchfulness of their many children. Again and again diaries and letters speak briefly of a child fallen into the campfire or under the wagon wheels: "All four wheels passed over his body. Small hope is held of his recovery." "Little Agnes B. fell into the fire today. Poorly." In the story of Narcissa Whitman, the first white woman to cross the Rocky Mountains, we learn about Catherine Sager, one of seven children whose father and mother both died on the long trail west. One day Catherine tripped on her skirt as she jumped from the family wagon and fell to the ground. A heavy wheel passed over her leg and broke it. She was badly lamed. And Catherine's mother, like the mother of Abigail Scott in the chapter called *The Prophet,* died beside the road giving birth to a new baby. These tragedies of a mother's death on the way west were only two out of many.

A one-day stopover for the birth of a child was all the time that could be spared. Emigrants were always racing with the weather, hoping to get over the Rocky Mountains before possible early storms set in. An unexpected delay might mean death in a blizzard or from slow starvation. Women in labor, or weak from birth, were expected to endure without complaint the racking motion of clumsy wagons on rough land.

Doctors were rarely found on wagon trains or in the early western settlements. Every woman had to learn and practice simple medicine herself. Bleeding was checked with cobwebs, or with wheat flour, or with salt in a poultice. Wet earth was applied to bites and stings, as were also scrapings from fresh vegetables, and bread and milk poultices. Sunflower seeds soaked in a pint of "spirits," allowed to stand for twelve hours and taken internally, were considered a sure cure for rheumatism. Whiskey too played a vital role in home medicine. It was freely prescribed for everything from inflammatory rheumatism to snakebite. Salt pork chopped up with onions served for attacks of what today we call tonsilitis. Onion syrup was a remedy beloved of all children for their winter colds. Today when we are beginning to learn more and more about the natural healing elements in things like mold, or onions, or tar, some of these old-fashioned remedies do not seem as foolish as they did a few years ago.

"People say to me," wrote an "old settler" at the turn of the century, " 'What did you do for a doctor?' We worked hard, ate hearty and slept sound. When we felt indisposed we took a tea made of wild cherry and dogwood bark and rested a while. The first doctor that came to our part of the country was Dr. Castro. Then the people began to get sick and they have wanted a doctor ever since."

Not all ailments, to be sure, yielded to wild cherry, dogwood bark and a short rest. Stories of the endurance of pain, or long-drawn-out sickness by these early emigrant women, are almost unbearable to read about. Yet some of these sufferers, all alone and desperately sick though they were, found the strength—perhaps even it *gave* them strength—to write about themselves in a diary: ". . . I am alone and no person who can take interest in my welfare to converse with and thus I have a great deal of time to think. I pray the Lord to uphold me and enable me to bear it [her pain] with more patience lest I wear my body down and become unable to raise my family."

During the periods of the great migrations frequent epidemics broke out on the trail: sometimes cholera, sometimes measles, sometimes an ailment that sounds very much like today's intestinal flu. When there was a death the burial had to be a brief and furtive one. Often because of pursuing Indians the emigrants dared not stop long enough to bury a corpse. At night a fire was built around the "dead wagon" because the stench of decaying flesh drew the wolves from miles around. After the body was finally laid in the earth the travelers drove their wagons over and over the spot to conceal the hiding place of their dear ones from marauding savages or hungry wolves. Then the wagon train pushed on.

Some of the Indians encountered along the way were friendly, others were not. Even when friendly their grotesquely painted faces, their half-naked bodies, their wild war whoops, their rough, husky, unintelligible speech must have been a nightmare to timid young girls and anxious mothers. Yet they all knew that they had to learn to live among the "Red people" when they finally came to rest. They could only pray that the Indians would remain peaceable. If they did not there was little hope of survival, for the Indians far outnumbered the whites in those early days.

Indians who were not hostile could be very troublesome too because of their great curiosity. They would stalk uninvited into a pioneer cabin and sit down by the fire to watch the odd activities of these strange pale-skinned women. They were particularly interested in the mystery of rising dough at bread-making times. They enjoyed poking their unwashed fingers into the strange white balloons.

When they were amiable, Indians were still not always welcome as visitors for they were often very

dirty and frequently had vermin. Narcissa Whitman, Mary Walker and Eliza Spalding, the first
missionary wives to travel to "Old Oregon," had to
stand by and permit friendly but often filthy Indians to hold their newborn infants in their arms.
Afterwards "in mortification" they would remove
lice from their babies' hair.

Stories of spunky women and thieving or just
plain annoying Indians often amaze us. At the end
of their patience these women would suddenly
chase Indians from their kitchens with brooms.
Fearless of consequences, they would slap their uninvited guests' hands as they would naughty children's when they were caught greedily reaching for
a freshly-baked pie: or they would scold them
soundly for not going home to help their own
squaws with the hard labor. There was a Lydia
Low of Washington Territory who caught a half-
naked Indian in the act of stealing a precious ham
from the rafters of her cabin. She was stirring a
large kettle of cornmeal mush when she saw him.
Without a moment's hesitation she snatched up the
large wooden spoon from the hot yellow meal and
applied it with vigor to the Indian's bare behind.
He did not linger and he left the ham.

Another woman who came of fighting Kentucky
stock dispersed single-handed a whole band of
thieving Indians who were unable to resist the
gleam of a bright kettle and the color of some gay
quilts hung out to air beside a camp. This nameless heroine snatched a tent pole out of the earth
and proceeded to lay it about her in all directions.
The Indians fled. The next day a chief turned up

to offer an apology, Indian style, for the behavior
of his young men. He also was prepared to offer
spot cash for the lady with the tent pole. He admired her spirit so greatly that he wished to make
her his wife.

Some women learned to shoot and some did not.
If they used a gun they prided themselves on not
handling a rifle in a "mannish way." Indeed
though the life was hard and exacted of them the
physical stamina of men, most pioneer women remained reassuringly feminine. They tried, as best
they could, to save some remnants of their youth
and good looks during the hot dry burning weeks
on the prairies and in the high mountains. The
deep scoop of their sunbonnets served them well
and nothing pleased a woman more than to be
told, just after she had crossed the plains, that she
wasn't in the least sunburned.

Against all rules, in secrecy or with mulish stub-
bornness, girls and women smuggled "useless"
things into the wagons, or argued long and hard
to be permitted to take certain articles their menfolk didn't understand. Mary Walker insisted on
carrying with her, to the wilderness, books about
plants and minerals. They proved extremely useful.
Abigail Scott smuggled a Webster's *Elementary Speller*
into her family's wagon. She remembered and told
about it years later when she founded a newspaper. One girl even managed to bring a wall
mirror from Ohio to the Pacific Coast. It became
a prized possession. Others brought not only seeds
for vegetable gardens but for flower gardens too.
They even tended precious slips from a sweet briar

or a trumpet vine they had sadly left behind shading a porch they were never to see again.

One of the things that maddened women most on the western trip was the endless dust and dirt. Some men complained that women in the wagon trains gave a lot of trouble because they were forever wanting to "stop and wash up" when they came to any pond, stream, lake or river. In the dry season the dust on the Oregon Trail rose as high and as thick as a wall in the wake of a passing company. The irritating alkaline powder filled the travelers' eyes, ears and nostrils. It sifted into their hair and onto their bodies even through their clothing. And there were many nights when there was no water in which to wash faces or hands before eating or sleeping.

Everyone on a wagon train had to do something useful if he was able to stand alone. Many young girls had the unpleasant job of walking behind the train to keep stray cattle from wandering. Can you imagine what the dust must have been like! One girl, just thirteen and a half, walked all the way from the Missouri River to the Willamette in western Oregon watching the cattle. She was the oldest of the six children in her family and there was no one else to do it. She made no complaints and in later years told her descendants her duties were "not deemed particularly hard when compared with those assigned to every other member of the train." Only babies and invalids were excused.

The long overland journey was not without moments of humor. We can read occasionally about bold young ladies who took to "the bloomer dress"

—certainly a sensible idea, but quite a shocking one in those days. We can almost hear one writer sniff as she takes up her pen to remark: "Met two of the bloomers at the river. . . . Mrs. Tait with a mind as changing as the wind has adopted the bloomer dress. . . . Two more bloomers this morning. Mrs. B. Allen and Miss Balbot. They are so tall they look very antick."

These independent-minded "bloomers" were the forerunners of the "Suffragettes" whom young Abigail Scott of the *Elementary Speller* was to find herself joining on a future day.

There were moments of gayety too en route to the farthest frontier. Old letters and diaries tell of wedding parties with brides' cakes made from turtle eggs happily found on a river bank. Sometimes, in spite of fatigue and anxiety, the emigrants would stop long enough to organize a dance and celebrate a birthday. A fiddler among them would get out his violin and play old square dances and familiar tunes for their pleasure:

> *Bird hop out and the Baboon in,*
> *Three hands round and you go agin.*

One can imagine them dancing in the moonlight on a stretch of flat green prairie, in sight at long last of the fabled Shining Mountains, the Indians' name for the towering snow-capped Rockies. They could not have guessed as they laughed and sang that the worst of the journey for many of them still lay ahead.

Some wagon trains had bad luck all the way. Some got through with comparative ease. The ones who got the breaks in weather and Indians, guides and good health, had only pleasant memories of the long trip. A few pioneers make it all sound a little like a trailer house journey of the present day. Here is one old lady's description of her covered wagon:

"On the centre cross-piece was placed a little round sheet-iron stove, about the size of a three-gallon bucket, with a little tea-kettle, a boiler and frying pan. On this little stove cooking was done with great ease and satisfaction. Mrs. Van Dusen says that many times she sat in her cosy little kitchen on wheels and cleaned and cooked a bird while the wagon moved along. On cold nights their little stove made their house very comfortable. They had also a little churn in the kitchen. The milk was placed in the churn each morning and the motion of the wagon churned it, so that every evening they had fresh butter. In this way one cow furnished them with sweet milk, buttermilk, and butter daily."

It can't be denied that occasionally girls and women got desperately homesick. On nights when it was raining and the day had been long and dull, when the road ahead seemed endless and the one behind lost forever, some young woman might take up a pen and write sad and touching lines like these found in an old diary: "Raining tonight. Looks rather dreary to me when it storms and I cast a thought upon that quiet little house that once sheltered us from wind and rain; but it is never to be seen again. . . ."

There was no turning back, and the women knew it, and thus there survive stories like those

of a Mrs. Longmire, one of a number of people who took an almost fatal "short cut" across the Cascade Mountains in 1853.

This group of emigrants—known in Northwest history as the Naches Party—came, in a state of exhaustion near their journey's end, to a high, very steep cliff down which it was impossible to drive their wagons.

After a conference they decided there was only one plan that could save them. They must kill some of their cattle, dry the hides and make enough ropes to lower thirty-six wagons over the steep cliff. The women and children would have to

scramble down the dangerous bluff as best they could.

All the women managed to make the descent without accident. One of them was Mrs. Longmire. She was walking a little ahead of the rest of the party on a narrow indistinct forest trail carrying a baby in her arms and leading a three-year-old by the hand. Suddenly there appeared before her, coming from the opposite direction, a grizzled trapper and fur trader. This "mountain man" hadn't seen a white woman in many years. He almost dropped dead of shock. When he could speak he cried out, "Good God Almighty, woman, where did you come from? Is there any more of you? You can't get through this way."

But it was obvious that they *were* coming through this way—women, children, men, wagons, cattle, oxen—all of them.

"You'll have to turn back," cried the trapper in horror. "There ain't a blade of grass for fifty miles," he warned.

Mrs. Longmire never faltered. She walked on past him, her face set resolutely westward. "We can't go back," she said. "We've got to go forward." And she went on walking the dark forest trail with her children, climbing over fallen logs, keeping a sharp eye out for bear and mountain lions.

When at last any group of these early emigrants decided that they had come as far as they could travel, or to some green place that appealed to them, they called a final halt. But after they had reached what some people with wry humor called "The Jumping Off Place itself" there was no rest for anybody. Everyone had to fall to immediately and make some kind of shelter.

Sometimes bad weather caught them early before they had any cabin built. Then they would have to spend the winter in a tent, or in a hole dug for a future cellar. One even reads about families in the land of the big trees clearing out an enormous tree stump, roofing it and moving in until spring. Often for many months, sometimes years, their houses had no doors or windows. Animal skins kept out the rain, snow and wind. The floor was simply hard-packed dirt. Cooking was done on an open hearth. Food had to be found right where they were. The wild game and berries, the fish and roots that the Indians themselves lived on became pioneer staples as well.

Where there was no corner store to supply her needs a woman had to develop her natural ingenuity as a provider of food, just as she had to experiment with homely medical cures in the absence of doctors.

Nobody knew anything about calories in those days but mothers were well aware that their children could not thrive on a straight diet of squash and berries, or salmon and boiled potatoes, or bread made of a "wheat" that consisted of cooked and mashed potatoes mixed with a little grain, parched in a skillet and ground in a coffee mill. Women were forever looking for something new to cook, or a new way to cook it. "Oh, dear," reads one amusing item in an old diary, "how can I tell it! Squash again for breakfast."

Some pioneers watched and learned from Indian women. They made bread as the squaws did from the camas root of the far western prairies. They succeeded in getting flour from the seeds of the great white water lilies that floated on the Klamath marshes in Oregon, or from certain fern roots, or the "wapato" roots that the squaws also deftly gathered with their toes in the river sloughs.

Some white people learned to cook, eat and enjoy a bulb which rather resembled the Jerusalem artichoke. They ate sunflower seeds and pumpkin seeds. They dried wild plums and grapes. They preserved wild blackberries or strawberries by thrusting them patiently, one at a time, into precious small-necked bottles. Sweets were very rare. There was little sugar, and to begin with not even honey, for domestic bees had to be brought all the way overland from the East. Milk was a great luxury. A woman who could not nurse her newborn child was sometimes in a dreadful plight. On the seacoast there were nourishing clams, and clam juice sometimes helped babies through the weaning period. It was also used to give invalids strength. But clams can become in time a somewhat monotonous diet. A wit from the State of Washington once remarked that during "hard times" the settlers of the Pacific Northwest had, of necessity, eaten so many clams that "their stomachs rose and fell with the tides."

Often a very simple statement in a diary, letter or story can make the picture of life in those days suddenly more vivid than paragraphs of description. A western grandmother told her grandchildren a story of a good neighbor in early Oregon who walked many miles to bring her a wonderful present. The present was a sack of old rags! "I never had a gift I prized as highly," she said. "There just wasn't any extra cloth to be had anywhere for all the uses rags are put to around a house."

It was when they reached the Jumping Off Place and their menfolk said, "Well, this looks like it to me," that women who had been fearless and tearless for many months sometimes broke down and had a good cry. Even little children could remember and tell later about the expressions on their mothers' faces at such times.

"I think I can see my mother's face now, with such a discouraged expression on it. She said then that she would have sold out for a picayune."

A first-hand account of the landing of the founders of Seattle at Alki Point describes such a scene:

"I can't never forget when the folks landed at Alki Point. I was sorry for Mrs. Denny with her baby and the rest of the women. . . . I remember it rained awful hard that last day—and the starch got took out of their bonnets and the wind blew, and when the women got into the rowboat to go ashore they were crying every one of them, and their sunbonnets with the starch took out of them went flip flap, flip flap, as they rowed off for shore, and the last glimpse I had of them was the women standing under the trees with their wet bonnets all lopping down over their faces and their aprons to their eyes."

But you may be sure they didn't stand there crying very long. They couldn't. There was too much to do. Tears and regrets and homesickness were luxuries in which no one could indulge for long at a time. These pioneer women had not walked or ridden many thousands of miles just to give way to sad memories. They had come west to help settle a wild land. First, then, there must be a house. After that a garden, then a school and a church. Then a little later, even before there were roads, the familiar American pattern these emigrants had known "at home" set itself up again: reading circles, debating societies, song fests, square dances, sewing bees, house raising, quilting bees, with people walking or riding miles and miles to have fun, help one another or just exchange ideas. Those widely separated "missionary ladies" of the very earliest Old Oregon days had organized their "Maternal Association" in order to discuss together, at their rare meetings, some of the problems of raising children in the uncivilized wilds.

And the history of the frontier period tells us too of meetings called in some forest clearing by fathers, husbands, and sweethearts, coming together to dispense "stump justice" or to pass necessary "frontier laws" in the absence of a definite governmental body of any kind. These meetings often began with the ringing American words, "We, the people" . . . Thus both the men and the women far from "home" reassured themselves of the democratic principles in which they had been brought up.

But also there was something new in the air out here on the Last Frontier—or so many of the women felt. Some new attitude towards women seemed to be evident. A cultivated New England lady, writing in the 1860s a story of Pacific Northwest travels almost as fabulous to her Boston friends as if she had been crossing Tibet, had this to say about her reception:

"Among the miners of the upper country, who had not seen a white woman for years, I received such honors that I am afraid I should have a very mistaken impression of my importance if I lived among them. At every stopping place they made

little fires in their frying-pans, and set them around me, to keep off the mosquitoes while I took my meal. As the columns of smoke rose about me, I felt like a heathen goddess, to whom incense was being offered."

In early Oregon for a few years, women were even permitted to own land in their own names. This was still unheard of elsewhere. As evidence of how much men wanted and needed women, Asa Mercer, a leading citizen of pioneer Seattle, actually chartered a ship, just after the Civil War, to bring a cargo of respectable girls all the way around the Horn—seven thousand miles—to the Pacific Coast. He didn't insult these girls by promising them husbands. (As if they couldn't get husbands where they were!) He just told them there were many useful things that they could do, most particularly teach school, for every western community was anxiously looking for schoolteachers for its children. Even married women had to lend their services if they had any qualifications at all, and so one can read pleasant reminiscences like this: "I taught the very first school until a regular teacher could be found. I rode horseback and carried my baby on the saddle in front of me. I remember this period as the happiest time of my life."

But if Asa Mercer talked about school teaching to the Eastern ladies he interviewed, he was perfectly direct with Western men. After his first successful experiment in bringing eleven charming girls to the Pacific Northwest, many local bachelors were anxious to help Mr. Mercer with a larger venture. The contracts he issued to men seeking

Eastern brides can still be read by anyone interested: "I, Asa Mercer, of Seattle, Washington Territory, hereby agree to bring a suitable wife of
good moral character and reputation from the East
to Seattle on or before September 1865, for each
of the parties whose signatures are hereunto at-
tached, they first paying to me or my agent the
sum of three hundred dollars, with which to pay
the passage of said ladies from the East and to
compensate me for my trouble."

Thoughtful Western women, observing what they
felt to be a new attitude towards their sex, tried
to analyze its source. Was it the pioneering adventure on which they, or their mothers, had embarked—some gladly, some unwillingly—that had
in some subtle way altered their status as "the
weaker sex"? For it was plain that they had
shown, in large numbers, a strength and a stamina
equal to a man's. As a matter of fact they had
shown even more marked courage and endurance.
As the bearers of children, the risks they ran on a
long overland journey into the farthest wilderness
were far greater than their husbands'.

Many stories were passed by word of mouth
among the early pioneers telling of the pluck and
spunk of certain women. One of the funniest was
told to his biographer (a woman) by Joe Meek,
the famous "mountain man" and fur trapper who
was to play a part, as we shall see, in the fateful
story of Narcissa Whitman.

Joe told about a certain Mrs. Smith, a missionary wife who, with her husband, somehow got

separated from the group with whom they were traveling west. The couple were found by Meek all alone on a barren, hot and dusty plateau in the Rocky Mountains. The woman was still on her feet holding the two horses, but the man lay prostrate on the ground groaning that he was "dying." Joe could see that Smith was not hurt anywhere but he knew that he *would* certainly die if he went on lying where he was in the hot sun. After trying to get him up without success, Joe made a strong, scornful speech:

"You're a damned pretty fellow to be lying on the ground there lolling your tongue out of your mouth and trying to die. Die, if you want to, you're of no account and will never be missed. Here's your wife, who you keep standing here in the hot sun; why don't she die? She's got more pluck than a white-livered chap like you."

Having delivered himself of these tough remarks with no apparent effect on Mr. Smith, Meek then tried to scare him by saying there were hostile Indians moving in their direction. Finally in desperation, Joe picked up Mrs. Smith—who was, you may be sure, quite terrified of this rough-bearded stranger. He put her in the saddle of one of the horses and shouted, "Ride!" He then set her horse going in the right direction with a good lash of a stick, jumped to his own saddle and rode off too. His parting shot to the man on the ground was, "Mrs. Smith can find plenty of better men than you." This final threat was effective. When Joe looked back a little distance down the trail he saw the "dying" man sitting up. That evening Mr.

Smith rode safely into camp. After this experience, however, it is not surprising to learn that he wrote back to the American Mission Board saying that the more he thought about it the more "improper" it seemed to him for females to travel across the plains! Fortunately nobody paid any attention to him.

The wife of another missionary, Mrs. Jason Lee, was left alone in the wilds among strangers to bear her first child while her husband took a long dangerous journey back to the East Coast. But she was brave enough, though filled with forebodings, to send him off with the cheerful words, "If you feel it your duty to go, go, for I did not marry you to hinder but to help you in your work." (Her forebodings came true. Both she and her baby died at the baby's birth.) And Narcissa Whitman, also left by her husband in the wilderness in the dead of winter, sick, exhausted, surrounded by sullen and angry Indians, begged him not to hurry back on her account. His duties came first, she said.

It wasn't that these women meekly submitted to their men, however, if they didn't agree with their ideas. "Why should I be afraid of Indians?" asked a certain Mr. Jackson of Washington Territory whose sensible wife was trying to persuade him to seek the shelter of the nearest fort. "I can load this gun quicker than you can run around the cabin," he boasted. "Can you, indeed?" said Mrs. Jackson, and she challenged him to prove it. His rifle was an old muzzle-loader, which required that the powder be tamped in with a piece of muslin.

She got the heaviest piece of cloth she could find in the cabin, handed it to him, and shot out the door. Round and round the cabin she ran, casting in glances from time to time to see how he was doing. Finally he admitted his defeat and they moved to the fort until the Indian trouble died down.

So, as you can see, there were many kinds of women from many different backgrounds, with quite different personalities, among these "heroines" of the early West. The majority of them are as nameless today as the little woman "no bigger'n a pint of cider" who walked over the Blue Mountains in a snowstorm carrying a baby and, on the far side, stopped beside the road long enough to give birth to another. Those women and girls who are not nameless to us a hundred years later are the ones who took the time and made the supreme effort to describe what they saw, thought, and felt during their great adventure. We particularly admire Narcissa Whitman, Mary Walker, Abigail Duniway and the Six Nuns from Namur, whose stories this book tells, because of what they have given us to read; the intimate personal records they left to posterity.

In an old faded book in a western library I once came upon a crude drawing of a woman in a calico sunbonnet standing on the top of a high mountain. Behind her and ahead could be seen the plodding oxen drawing those great lumbering "prairie schooners" that moved like slow white sails across the "dry sea" of the plains in the last century. Far out of sight behind this nameless woman one could imagine the familiar comforts she had given up "back home," hundreds, even thousands, of miles away. Ahead of her, down the steep rocky slope that pitched towards the distant Pacific, there lay the Great Unknown. Yet this woman does not look afraid, and the caption under the picture reads proudly, "Woman, yes, *woman*, has come over the top of the world!"

CHAPTER TWO

SACAJAWEA

$\mathcal{T}$HE white women who came overland by horse and wagon or on foot, or who traveled a long dangerous journey by sea around the Horn in order to settle a new and unknown land, could never have played their historic roles if it had not been for a young Indian woman named Sacajawea. This young Indian, a captured Shoshone "slave," deserves to be honored among "the greatest women in American history." So says a famed historian, James Truslow Adams, who, as an elector of our Hall of Fame, nominated her to a place among the heroes and heroines of our country.

Sacajawea, or Bird Woman as she is sometimes called, won this high honor because of the help she gave the first official expedition sent out from the capital of the then young United States to explore an unmapped continent. This was the Lewis and Clark Expedition which, in the years 1804 to

1806, crossed America as far as the north Pacific coast and then came back to report its findings to President Jefferson—an important exploration that proved to be one of several factors helping the young United States claim the far western lands.

It now seems clear that without the guidance and aid of this little Shoshone "squar," Sacajawea, the twenty-nine adventurous members of the historic band might not have won through to the Pacific coast.

The first public recognition of Sacajawea's services came long after her death. It was in the year 1905 that a statue of her was unveiled in Portland, Oregon, at the Lewis and Clark Exposition—one hundred years after these two famous heroes and their followers had reached the Pacific shores. The speech at the statue's unveiling was made by a woman, another pioneer. This was none other than Abigail Scott Duniway, the girl, who smuggled Webster's *Elementary Speller* into the family's covered wagon and who, as a woman, founded a newspaper and became that dreaded creature, a "Suffragette." In her speech Abigail honored Sacajawea as a "symbol of all the unsung and unrewarded virtues of frontier womankind." Today there are other statues in other Far Western towns also honoring the little guide dressed in her elkskin clothes and boots, her long hair in braids over her shoulders, her papoose strapped to her back.

It was not much more than a hundred and fifty years ago when Meriwether Lewis and William

Clark were sent by President Jefferson to explore
and report on that vast stretch of mysterious land
lying west and north of the Mississippi River.

When you look at a map today it seems hard to
imagine that all that great stretch of western country, now so thickly dotted with the names of towns
and cities, was once as free of all landmarks as a
large stretch of fresh white tablecloth. The western
United States—not yet a part of the States at all
—was, as has already been mentioned, quite as
"foreign" as any distant land overseas. Much less
was known about this part of America than we
know today about sections of darkest Africa or re-
motest Manchuria.

In the year 1804, Lewis and Clark with twenty-nine hand-picked followers were camping on the Missouri River trying to find an interpreter to accompany them and translate for them among the hostile Indians to the north and west.

The interpreter Lewis and Clark finally chose was a French and Indian half-breed named Charbonneau. Charbonneau had a young pure-blooded Indian wife named Sacajawea.

By birth, Sacajawea belonged to the Shoshone tribe. She had been captured in a raid by enemy Indians and sold into captivity as a slave. It was said that her husband had won her as a prize in a gambling game.

Wherever he got her it was plain Charbonneau did not want to lose her. He insisted that she must go with him on the long western adventure. Since Charbonneau would not leave her behind and Lewis and Clark needed his services as interpreter, they finally had to give in to his demand.

They agreed with reluctance to allow Sacajawea to accompany them. It was a very lucky day for them, but they did not yet know it. Even though she was an Indian "squar" and used to the hardships of primitive travel, they feared she would prove a problem and a burden in the many strenuous months ahead. The fact that she was carrying a papoose strapped to her back presented a particular difficulty in their minds. She would have to carry this child all the way across the continent and back again, and on the return journey the infant would be at the toddling stage and a much heavier load.

However, since there was no way to hire Charbonneau without taking his wife too, Sacajawea and her baby joined the little band of intrepid white men. It was not long before the kindly, redheaded William Clark had decided not to try to pronounce Sacajawea in the proper style but to call the little Indian "Janey" instead. As for the papoose who had been given by his proud father the French name, Baptiste, Clark chose to call him "Pompey." And as "Little Pomp" the baby was known to all the men on the long grueling journey that was to last almost two and a half years, during which every kind of danger and hardship, including at one point near starvation, was to be experienced by the entire party.

They were only a short distance out on their great overland adventure when Sacajawea won the undying gratitude of Lewis and Clark by an act of singular cool-headedness.

The expedition had come by boat to the upper reaches of the Missouri River. Sacajawea was riding in the lead canoe with her baby, little black-eyed "Pompey." In the same canoe were the expedition's surveying instruments, maps, medicine and other vital supplies. A squall struck without warning and since the canoe was at the time carrying sail, it keeled over dangerously. Charbonneau, who was guiding this crude bateau, completely lost his head. Amid wild cursing, shouting and general pandemonium the boat all but capsized.

Although Sacajawea had herself and her baby to save, she was also aware of the importance of the lead canoe's equipment. With extraordinary courage, quick thinking, and quicker action, she managed to snatch from the swirling current the most precious papers and supplies just as they were washed overboard.

That night in his journal, Clark acknowledged their tremendous debt to the Indian woman. They were already 2,200 miles from home and the sources of their necessary equipment. Had it been lost in the river that day, the expedition would have faced disaster. They would have had to turn back and start all over again and the delay might well have cost the United States the loss of the lands of the far Northwest, for Great Britain also had her shrewd eye on them. (In the end it was to be nip and tuck as to whether they would become British or American.)

Sacajawea proved indispensable to this historic expedition in many other ways as well. She knew, for instance, the hidden foods of the unexplored western land. She was able to find the delicious wild artichoke hearts stored by gophers in their prairie holes. She knew where wild carrot, wild fennel, and the far western "wapato" or wild potato would be growing, and she would dig for their roots to put in soups. She knew how to break and boil the shank bones of elk and other wild animals to extract the nourishing marrow.

All this was of the greatest value since the matter of getting proper food in the wilderness was of first importance. Men living too long on unbroken diets of salt fish, jerked meat and rough bread often developed dietary troubles and became too sick and weak to travel. As it was, there were many times on the long journey when Lewis and Clark and their men had only tallow candles to eat; nothing else at all. This was when winter weather caught them high in the mountains with no game to be found.

The Journals of the expedition kept by Lewis and Clark reveal Sacajawea's many remarkable qualities. They tell us, for instance, of her unflinching courage. On one hunting expedition Charbonneau, Lewis, Sacajawea and Little Pomp were caught in a sudden flood and nearly drowned. Lewis lost his compass. It was the only one the expedition had. He dived into the water over and over again hoping to recover it. And who dived with him? Not Charbonneau but Sacajawea. The little squaw, who had learned the importance of this magic instrument whose needle always pointed mysteriously to the north, dived and swam until she became exhausted trying to find the compass where it had fallen. Neither she nor Clark succeeded in their efforts. The expedition had to go on without this most valuable piece of equipment.

Sacajawea knew many other ways to be useful, too. She could mend the men's clothes with her needles of small bird bones, her thread of fiber and hide. She could even provide them with leather moccasins when their own stout shoes gave out on the rough trails. Together with two men of the party she made 338 moccasins for the long return journey from the Pacific Ocean to St. Louis.

But perhaps the most important of all her natural gifts was her unerring sense of direction. Lewis and Clark had only a rough, rather inaccurate elk-hide map of the western region to guide them. Sacajawea, however, possessed an ability that seemed to the white men almost uncanny. She would look at a row of distant mountains that appeared to them only as a jagged ridge of blue on the distant sky and, as if by instinct, she would seem to know just where the hidden passes lay. Streams and rivers also yielded to her the secret of their distant sources.

There had been many weary days and weeks of unbroken travel when at last the little group came to the natural barrier known as the Great Divide. This was the place where the waters of streams and rivers no longer flowed eastward towards the homes the white men had left so far behind them, but westward instead towards the setting sun and the farthest wilderness.

Soon Sacajawea found herself again in the landscape of her childhood. One of the first landmarks she recognized were strange red clay banks so curiously shaped that the expedition named them "The Beaverhead Rocks," thinking that they resembled mountain beaver. The bright crimson clay of these banks, Sacajawea told them, was used by her people to make their war paint. War paint! This was hardly a reassuring thought for the travel-worn expedition, not sure yet whether the Shoshones would prove friends or enemies.

Though Sacajawea let them know they had reached Shoshone country, they saw no signs of any Indians. Yet they were uneasily aware that they were being watched by invisible eyes. Once in a while they did catch sight of distant smoke signals rising into the clear sky. What were the signals saying? They did not know. One day Clark's quick eye saw moccasin tracks in a damp place on the trail. They knew then that the Indians were near by. But still they did not see any of them. It was an uncanny fearful feeling to be spied on secretly by possible hidden enemies.

It was Sacajawea who suggested one night that they make a fire and leave on a rock near it some blue beads, a looking glass, and a knife for cutting out moccasins. This would show their friendly intentions to any Indians who might be lurking about watching them from rocks and bushes as they plodded westward.

After they laid the offerings on the rock, they all stole away and slept some distance off.

In the morning the offerings were gone. But still no Indians appeared.

At last there came a day when they heard the sound of many horses' hoofs far in the distance. In a short time a band of sixty Shoshones in full regalia of paint and feathers appeared on the horizon. Every heart stood still. Every man fastened his hand on his rifle and waited tensely. The Indians numbered two to their one.

The chieftain heading the Indian party rode with impressive dignity towards Lewis, who was walking slowly, guardedly towards the Shoshones.

Suddenly Sacajawea gave a loud glad cry and darted forward from among the white men. To the amazement of them all they saw the Shoshone chief himself dismount and then they saw their little squaw "Janey" throw her blanket over him and burst out weeping. It was Sacajawea's brother Cameahwait whom she had not seen since she was captured many years before in the raid by the Blackfeet that had made her a slave.

This chance encounter with Cameahwait was the greatest possible piece of good fortune for Lewis and Clark. Through the influence of this powerful chief they would be able to get the horses they

must have in order to travel on through the mountains to the shores of the Pacific Ocean.

Cameahwait was very much impressed with the
position of honor his sister enjoyed among such important envoys from the Great White Father in
Washington. To his pride in his sister there was
also added gratitude when she was able to bestow
on him, from the expedition's meager stores, gifts of
food that he had never so much as seen before.
These were white men's luxuries, sugar, squash,
corn and beans.

Shrewd Sacajawea knew what importance gifts
of food would have for the Shoshones. A wandering tribe with no knowledge of agriculture, they
were never free of the pressing problem of finding
enough to eat for all their people. No gift could
have been more welcome than these delicacies to
these particular Indians, with their unvarying diet
of buffalo, fish, wild roots and mountain berries.

Impressed and grateful, Cameahwait agreed to
ask his people to postpone their annual buffalo-
hunting expedition until they had led Lewis and
Clark and Sacajawea over the Great Divide. In return, so Sacajawea told the Shoshones, the Great
White Father, President Jefferson, would help them
to hunt for game farther south than usual without
danger from enemy tribes. Also someone would
soon come to teach them to grow their own beans
and squash and corn. What was more, the Great
White Father would establish trading posts nearby
and there the Shoshones could get guns to make
hunting easier for them.

Although most of the Shoshones were willing to aid the friendly white men, there remained a few hostile ones who began to mutter among themselves. If they delayed in order to conduct the white men over the mountains, snow would surely come and they would miss the buffalo, their chief source of food for the winter.

A plot was secretly hatched to lead the white party into the mountains and there abandon them.

Once again Sacajawea came to the rescue. She discovered the treachery in time to warn Lewis and Clark.

Perhaps it was at her advice that they then staged a great entertainment for the Indians with pipe-smoking, dancing and singing. The expedition had brought along a fiddler named Cruzatte. Cruzatte and his fiddle had often helped to cheer the men when they grew weary, dispirited or homesick in the long exile from their families.

Now Cruzatte got out his fiddle to entertain the Indians. He played old country tunes and all the men danced the Virginia Reel and the Irish Jig.

Then York, the Negro, danced too: cakewalks, clogs and shuffles. The Indians, who had never seen a Negro, were delighted with York.

After a while the Indians rose and also danced, beating the earth with their moccasined feet and chanting their eerie songs that sounded like rising winds.

At last the pipe of peace was brought out, lit and passed from hand to hand. Good will and friendship were pledged. The expedition went on at

last over the Rocky Mountains and eventually
down into the unknown land where the fabled
Oregon River, now called the Columbia, rolled on
its way to the Pacific Ocean.

But even after leaving her own people, the Shoshones, Sacajawea's usefulness was not yet at an
end. She went right on helping the men tend the
sick, find food, mend their clothes, make new garments of elk skin.

At the Christmas of 1805, spent at Clatsop in the present state of Washington, when all the homesick party tried to give gifts to one another and celebrate the day as best they could in the rainy wilderness, Sacajawea presented Captain Clark, the cheerful redhead who seems to have been her favorite, with twenty-four skins of the whitest ermine. She had carried them with her hidden under her garments all the way from Fort Mandan, many hundreds of miles back on the journey.

Over and over again Sacajawea's presence averted trouble. Since among western Indians no war party ever took women with them on raids, when the Far Western tribes saw Sacajawea it was proof to them that the white strangers' intentions were peaceful.

She was still proving useful too as an interpreter near the shores of the Pacific Ocean. Some of the difficulties of communication with Indians of unknown language can be imagined from an entry made in one of the expedition's *Journals:*

"In the first place we spoke in English to one of our men who translated it into French to Charbonneau; he interpreted it to his wife in the Minnetaree language and she then put it into Shoshonee, and the young Shoshonee prisoner explained it to the Chopunnish in their own dialect."

There is no record anywhere in the journals of any complaint on Sacajawea's part, or any flagging of her energies. She was at one time sick—but so, for that matter, were all the men of the expedition in those months of deprivation. When she fell ill she was tenderly cared for. They all valued her now. She slept in the main tent.

For her services in the two and a half years of hardship, Sacajawea asked only one "indulgence": she begged to go with the men to view the "Big Water," the Pacific Ocean. Lewis and Chief Red Head, as she called Clark, permitted her to come along.

Sacajawea's awe at the sight of the ocean, however, was lost in her amazement at the carcass of a whale cast up on the Pacific sands. In later years she told her "fish story" to hundreds of inland Indians, and when she measured out quite accurately from hitching post to tepee the whale's great length, they would yell with joy at her "big lie." At the same time she would describe her first sight of the seals she had seen on the Oregon shore as "people who lived in the water" with no one doubting the story at all!

As for her baby, "Little Pomp," Captain Clark gave him an education in St. Louis and he grew

up to be an interpreter and a traveler like his mother—with one big difference. Baptiste was paid for *his* work! Baptiste acted as guide and interpreter for expeditions of rich European noblemen who came all the way by slow boat across the Atlantic to see, in the early days of the frontier, the wild country and the strange aboriginal natives before civilization had altered the picture.

Sacajawea, who lived to be more than one hundred years of age, kept on traveling too. She crossed the western country many times as an old woman on the free passes with which early stage-coach companies provided her. Wherever she went she acted as an unpaid agent of good will for the white people. Known among Indians by a variety of names—Chief, Lost Woman, Great Woman— she spent the remainder of her long life spreading good feeling between the Americans and the people of her own race. In the days when the buffalo were fast disappearing it is said she did her best to persuade the Plains Indians to change their wandering way of life, settle down to learn agriculture and enjoy a peaceful existence.

Since her death in 1884, Sacajawea's fame has grown steadily. The monuments raised in her honor in Far Western towns salute the intelligence, courage and kindness of an Indian woman who played a part in saving for the young United States the great natural riches and beauties of the country where the states of Montana, Idaho, Washington and Oregon now appear on our maps.

In all her wandering with the men of the Lewis and Clark Expedition, she had traveled on foot through an area that comprises not only part of the four Far Western states just named but of large parts of Kansas, Iowa, Nebraska, South Dakota, North Dakota, and Wyoming as well.

If you mark on a map the area on which these brave men and this equally brave little Indian woman tramped—often in danger of violent death, frequently hungry, sometimes even starving, footsore, anxious, exhausted but always *determined*—you will agree that Sacajawea does, indeed, belong in our Hall of Fame.

CHAPTER THREE

FIRST WHITE WOMAN ACROSS
THE ROCKIES

*T*HERE is a special kind of radiance around the name of Narcissa Whitman, the first white woman to cross the "impassable barrier" of the Rocky Mountains in the year 1836, thirty-two years after Sacajawea helped to guide Lewis and Clark.

Narcissa was born with all the qualities proper to a heroine of a great drama. Beautiful, intelligent, gifted, the daughter of an eminent father and a fine mother, she traveled as a bride with her doctor husband, Marcus, all the way from upstate New York across the fabled American continent to make a home among unknown Indians in what is now the state of Washington.

Eleven years after she had set out with such courage and high hopes, Narcissa was brutally murdered, along with Marcus, by the very Indians they had hoped to "save."

The circumstances of this martyrdom, which helped to make people along the Eastern seaboard and in the nation's capital suddenly aware of the Far West, have, in part, contributed to Narcissa's fame. But not all of our interest in this remarkable woman stems from her tragic fate. Narcissa had the gift of words. She left, for later generations to read, a journal and a number of long and detailed letters. Through her simple but clear and moving phrases we come to know a great deal about how she felt and thought and what she experienced during the great adventure that was to cost her her life.

If a woman like Narcissa Prentiss Whitman was to set out today on such an "unheard of journey" to an unexplored land where no other white woman had ever set foot, it is easy to imagine the kind of coverage her story would get in newspapers and magazines, on radio and television. All the details of how such a heroine looked, what she wore, what she took along with her and how she felt about her future, would become public property.

Although Narcissa's departure aroused a good deal of stir in her little community in upstate New York it passed, otherwise, almost unnoticed. Means of communication in the year 1836 were not at all what they are today. Indeed poor Narcissa, who loved her friends and family dearly, was to live in the Far West for two years and five months without hearing a single word from anyone at home!

There was no postal system across the continent in those days. Letters had to be passed from hand to hand among trappers and traders, and the chance of reaching their destination was a slim one. Mail often went off addressed simply to "So-

and-So, West of the Rocky Mountains" or "So-
and-So, trapper, on the River Ouregon." If the letters went by sea they were almost equally subject
to loss or delays, for that was long before the Pan-
ama Canal had been built as a short cut from the
East to the West Coast. Ships from eastern seaports
had to sail the long, slow, hazardous way around
the tip of South America in order to reach the
West Coast. Mail out of Boston often came to the
Pacific via London or even Canton, China. The
islands of Hawaii, then known as the Sandwich
Islands, were considered "neighbors" of the few
scattered settlers in the isolated Northwest.

Narcissa Whitman, born Narcissa Prentiss, would
certainly, however, have proved good copy for any
reporter who had been around to cover this first
overland journey by a white woman. The daughter
of an "Honorable"—Judge Stephen Prentiss—she
possessed most of the stock attributes of glamour in
the early nineteenth century or, for that matter, in
any century, including our own. She had golden
hair, a "voice sweet and musical as a chime of
bells . . . a splendid carriage . . . very graceful de-
portment . . . with a brilliant sparkling eye"—so
her friends described her. Altogether here was a
combination of physical attributes which was to
bring her, as she journeyed westward, the flattering
attention of certain rough fur trappers, some of
whom had not seen a civilized white woman for
twenty-five years.

Besides her physical charms, Narcissa had a good
mind and, unlike most girls of her day, she had

been given an education. She had even attended Mrs. Emma Willard's select Female Seminary in Troy, New York, where she had also learned certain graces of manner pleasing to all she met. As a young schoolteacher she had shown exceptional ability and courage by attempting to instruct her pupils in a mysterious subject called "chemistry" and another, even more difficult, known then as "natural philosophy" which today we call "physics."

Narcissa's exceptional mind and spirit had outgrown the narrow confines of upstate village life by the time she was sixteen. In the early nineteenth century, however, there was little hope for escape into a larger world except by an unusual marriage or by going as a missionary to "heathen lands." Narcissa had tried hard to be accepted as a missionary but, as other women like her were to find out in the years just ahead, single women were not acceptable as missionaries except in "boarding schools." There were certainly no boarding schools among the Western Indians!

Narcissa might never have gone west had it not been for her chance meeting with young Marcus Whitman.

The romance of Narcissa and Marcus was helped along by a traveling preacher named Samuel Parker who had come through the highways and byways of New York State in 1834 telling people about the Redman's wish for the "Black Book" or "the Book of Heaven," which was the Bible. Dr. Parker told his congregations about the Indians' desire for missionary teachers to come and preach to them about the Christian faith. Who would dare accept this great challenge?

Both Marcus and Narcissa—in their separate communities—heard Dr. Parker speak and they both longed to follow him west and give their lives to "the savages." Marcus was a doctor of medicine, not of divinity, but he did know something about preaching, and he also thought that his knowledge of medicine might prove helpful in "civilizing" those distant unknown Indians.

By a fateful chance Marcus and Narcissa met. They found they shared the same dreams and hopes. They fell in love and got engaged.

As soon as they were engaged Marcus went off with Dr. Parker on an exploring trip as far as the Rocky Mountains. Narcissa had begged to be married and go west with him at once, but Marcus was cautious. He wanted to see whether it was really possible for a delicate woman to make the difficult overland journey. He came back convinced that it was and he and Narcissa were immediately married in the little town of Angelica where her family, the Prentisses, were then living.

Had that imaginary reporter happened to be in Angelica on the day of the Prentiss-Whitman wedding ceremony, he could have written a most dramatic account of what went on. For some reason that has never been explained Narcissa got married in a black bombazine dress—the color and material used for mourning. All her female relatives wore black also. Were they already mourning Narcissa's death? For it was, in a way, her death

to them. She never expected to—nor did she—see any of them again. Yet when all her friends and family broke down in the singing of the last hymn, Narcissa's beautiful clear soprano carried through bravely to the end. No matter how she was feeling inside, she was strong enough to sing all the words of the famous missionary hymn which began,

Friends, connections, happy country.
Can I bid you all farewell,
Can I leave you
Far in heathen lands to dwell?

By another most curious turn of fate, Narcissa and Marcus were to travel west and take up life in the same section of the vast wilderness with two other young missionaries from New York State, Henry and Eliza Spalding. Henry Spalding was a rejected suitor of Narcissa's who had never quite recovered from the fact that she had turned him down. This was to cause some strife and heart-burning later when Henry could not keep from making sharp criticisms about the woman he had once wished to marry. So well known was Henry's resentful attitude toward Narcissa, and so thoroughly did Narcissa's father understand his temperament, that Judge Prentiss had thought it wise —once he learned the two couples were bound for the frontier together—to call Henry to his study and plead with him to keep himself in hand. Henry made promises. He also tried to keep them, but he was not always successful.

Henry's wife Eliza, however, was a "saint," as Narcissa said, and this must have helped to relieve the tensions a little. About Eliza we know much less than we do about Narcissa because Eliza was not a writer. But we do know that she must have been a woman of boundless courage. Frail and plain, sickly but plucky, she had just lost a child before she set out westward and was really too much of an invalid to go. But since she did not want to cause her husband any delay in his missionary career, she started off valiantly on the seven months' journey.

Horseback riding was agony to Eliza. So, for that matter, was the jolting wagon the two men were trying to take overland—to prove that it could be done. (A most important piece of propaganda for possible future settlers, as Marcus clearly saw.)

Eliza could not digest buffalo meat or any other of the rough foods that made up the travelers' monotonous diet. At one point, worn out with sickness, exhaustion and hunger, she begged the others to go on and leave her. "Do not put me on that horse again," she pleaded. But when she saw that they would not leave and that she was thus endangering their lives also, she got back on the horse once more and plodded wearily westward.

Although Eliza needed Marcus's medical skills all the way to Oregon, Narcissa fortunately was in the best of health. Like many women who were to follow her in the next thirty years, she had become pregnant on the journey west, but she had no sickness and could even eat horse meat when she had to "with good relish." She was in love and happy; constantly excited over the great adventure on which she was embarked, the day after day of movement through an unfamiliar world, the nameless unknown at the end of the journey.

The Whitmans and Spaldings traveled in the company of the fur caravan that went out of St. Louis every year to the Rocky Mountains to trade necessary supplies in exchange for the valuable furs the "mountain men" and Indians had been gathering all year. The men of this fur caravan were rough and "godless." They swore, drank, had Indian mates, refused to keep the Sabbath, gambled, fired off guns, whooped and hollered and in gen-

eral carried on in a manner for which Narcissa
and Eliza were totally unprepared.

But the two carefully-reared white women had
to accept their crude traveling companions just as
they found them. More than that, they had to be
grateful, for without these rough men who knew
every trail and water hole, every mountain pass
and river ford, and all about Indians, the missionaries could never have found their way to Oregon.
And they knew it.

For that matter the men of the caravan would
never have permitted the unwelcome company of
"pious" missionaries, and "squeamish" white women
from gentle backgrounds, had it not been for something that happened when Marcus first went west
with Dr. Parker.

A famous "mountain man" named Jim Bridger
had heard that a "sawbones" was traveling through
the buffalo country with a "Reverend." Jim Bridger
decided to take himself to the doctor and ask him
if he could remove an arrowhead embedded in his
back many years before by an Indian warrior.
Marcus had agreed to try. There was, of course,
no anaesthetic. Jim Bridger took a big swig of
whisky, lay down flat on his face and Marcus, in
the midst of an interested audience of trappers,
traders and Indians, had managed to remove the
arrowhead. (Bridger was so grateful that he later
sent his little half-breed daughter to the mission
school that Narcissa founded in the western wilderness.)

After the operation on Bridger other mountain

men and even Indians had come to Marcus with
their wounds and their embedded arrowheads. Thus
the news of his skill as a surgeon traveled by word
of mouth through the western lands. And when he
turned up a second time in St. Louis, now with a
bride and two missionary companions, the caravan
was willing to let him join them.

Although Narcissa, on the whole, enjoyed the
western journey, she must have had bad moments
of homesickness as the miles stretched out ever
farther and farther behind her. Certainly she had
to endure with patience many discomforts and
many hardships. Much of the trip was also un-
avoidably monotonous, even boring. Once in a letter home, she speaks of lingering behind the rest of
the company to be alone with "husband" to talk of
family and friends and things given up forever: "It
is then the tedious hours are sweetly decoyed
away," she wrote. And again, near the journey's
end, at Fort Walla Walla, the first settled community they had seen in many months, Narcissa
wrote in such a way about the appearance of a
rooster on the doorstep that a reader is suddenly
aware of the sharp contrast between her present
life and what she had known before:

"While at breakfast a young rooster placed himself upon the sill of the door and crowed. Now
whether it was the sight of the first white woman,
or out of compliment to the company, I know not,
but this much for him: I was pleased with his appearance. You may think me simple for speaking

of such a small circumstance. No one knows the feelings occasioned by seeing objects once familiar after a long deprivation."

With these words about a rooster one looks through the eyes of a sheltered young woman from a gentle New York countryside, at her fabulous. journey through an untouched land. Endless plains with great herds of buffalo. Towering snow-capped mountains, roaring rivers, and impenetrable forests. The strange company of uncouth men, the ever-present threat of hostile Indians and the tactless intimacies of friendly ones (at some stops Indian women had all but smothered Narcissa with embraces). The unremitting toil and hardship of fording turbulent rivers, climbing rocky slopes, riding every day in all weather to the point of exhaustion at a pace set by toughened male travelers.

Narcissa sang a lot on that western trip and she tried to teach Marcus to carry a tune too. She hoped her singing might prove helpful in getting Indians to come and listen to her husband preach, for at stopovers along the way, whenever she sang, Indians as well as whites would gather to listen in awe to her golden voice. Joe Meek, that famous mountain man, was never to forget the impression made on him by this first civilized and gracious woman he had encountered in many years of rough life, far from the respectable home he had known as a boy down South.

In general men were apt to offer Narcissa flattering attentions. In her journal, *A Journey Across the Plains in 1836,* she tells of a certain Mr. McLeod who made for her—and Eliza also—"fried cakes as a treat," lent Narcissa his big horse to swim a deep river and, when they neared Fort Walla Walla, galloped on ahead just to bring her a muskmelon a few hours early.

Fort Walla Walla was the first real rest the two women had had since leaving home. After a brief pleasant change of scene and company at this Fort there was an even more delightful interlude at Fort Vancouver farther west on the Columbia River. Here Eliza and Narcissa were guests of the famous Dr. John McLoughlin, a high-living factor of the mighty Hudson's Bay Company of Great Britain— a company which at that time pretty well ruled the American wilderness. Dr. McLoughlin greatly admired the two white women. He spoke openly of their "heroism" and he set himself to make their respite at Vancouver a memorable one.

While Marcus and Henry went up the Columbia River to find their mission sites, Narcissa and Eliza remained at the Fort where they were treated as though they were great dignitaries. Narcissa wrote her family about how the gentlemen of the Fort toasted them nightly in wine (not without embarrassing them as they belonged to the "TeeTotal Society"). She also described at length the kind of food they got here; a far richer fare than she had been accustomed to even back in civilized New York State. Roast duck was an everyday dish, also salmon, sturgeon, boiled pork and tripe. There were fancy desserts and delicious fruits from the factor's own gardens—for McLoughlin, who was known among the Indians as The White-Headed Eagle, lived like a veritable King of the Wilderness. He even had a kilted Highland bagpipe player to "pipe" him in to dinner every night like a real Scottish laird. What impressed Narcissa particularly about the meals, however, was not alone the richness and variety of the food but the fact that with every course the entire company was given a fresh plate. And she did not have to do the dishes!

Marcus and Henry had decided on the sites of their two missions. They were one hundred and twenty miles apart, a vast distance for those days and certainly a foolhardy idea in an unsettled land among unknown Indians. (This seems to have been Henry's idea. Perhaps he did not want to be too near Narcissa whom he had plainly not yet quite plucked out of his heart.)

Henry's mission site was at a spot called Lapwai on the Clearwater River, now in the state of Idaho. His Indians were the agreeable Nez Perces. Marcus chose a place on Cayuse land, not far from present-day Walla Walla in the state of Washington. The name of the site Marcus chose—a name to become famous in the annals of Indian massacre— was Waiilatpu, which meant in the local Indian tongue "place of the rye grass." The land seemed fertile for future gardens. There was a stream where he could build a gristmill. There was plenty of timber around: cottonwood, birch, balm of Gilead and thorn, with pine on the mountain slopes about fifteen miles distant.

As soon as the two men had decided on the sites for their future homes, Marcus came back down the Columbia River to pick up Narcissa and

Eliza. Dr. McLoughlin tried to persuade Narcissa
to remain at the Fort at least until the time of
her child's delivery. He had a kind and intelligent
Indian wife who could assist her and she would be
sure of shelter, food, comforts—even luxuries—and
safety at all times. But she refused the invitation
of this "most sympathetic man," as she called him.
She was anxious to get to her future home. In a
pouring rain she and Eliza set off with Marcus up
the wide and treacherous river in a small open
boat while John McLoughlin stood on the shore
watching them go and shaking his noble white
head in misgiving.

Though Marcus did not realize it, he had invited disaster when he chose to settle among the
Cayuses. At first, when there had been hot com-
petition among the various Indian tribes over the
honor of having, on their own land, these strange
white people who had come not to trade but to
preach, the Cayuses had begged hard for the privilege of being the Whitmans' hosts. Yet it was not
long before Narcissa was writing home that a Cayuse chief named Umtippe was "full of all manner
of hypocrisy, deceit and guile." He had even gone
so far as to demand that the missionaries must pay
the Cayuses for learning to speak the Cayuse language!

The Indians did not like to be told by Marcus
that they must lead a different kind of life if they
hoped for "salvation." Narcissa wrote that "One
said it was good when they knew nothing but to
hunt, eat, drink and sleep; now it was bad." They

threatened to whip Marcus. They even put their horses into a newly planted potato field every night hoping to change his attitude toward them. The Spaldings, living among the more intelligent and tractable Nez Perces, were having no such problems as these.

But when, to the Whitmans' joy, Narcissa was delivered of a beautiful blonde baby girl whom they named Alice Clarissa after her Whitman and Prentiss grandmothers, Indian feelings took a change for the better. The Cayuses were thrilled with the arrival of this blue-eyed, white-skinned baby. They all wanted to hold her and look at her in wonder. None among them was more delighted than Tilaukait, one of the eventual murderers. He told the Whitmans that they should name the child "Cayuse *te-mi* (girl) because she was born on Cayuse *wai-tis*" (ground).

The company of her child was a source of great happiness to Narcissa, left alone so much while Marcus was away among the Indians. It seemed to lighten the endless drudgery and worries that now filled her days. For the Whitmans not only had to make their own living quarters by hand, with the crudest of means, they also must build a school and a place of worship. They must teach the Indians, against quickly growing opposition, the simplest fundamentals of cleanliness and morality— white style. They wished also to teach them to till the soil in order to grow their own crops, something these Indians had never done before. The Cayuses' very lives depended on the amount of

game and fish they could get in any season, and
in years of bad weather, when game was scarce,
they often starved.

At the end of two years of unceasing labor nine
other missionaries came into this part of Oregon.
(Among them was Mary Walker whom we shall
read about in another chapter.) The arrival of
these missionaries, though a source of comfort to
the Whitmans, laid many more cares and domestic
duties on Narcissa, for, to begin with, all the newcomers had to crowd into the small quarters at
Waiilatpu.

Sometimes in these cramped quarters, surrounded
by strangers and bands of ever-curious Indians,
Narcissa lost her patience. Sometimes she gave way
to fits of weeping. But she was always repentant
afterwards, humbly apologized and asked forgive-
ness for her "short-comings." Narcissa longed to be
"good." She was given to self-analysis, as her writ-
ings clearly show: "I find one of my most difficult
studies is to know my own heart, the motive by
which I am actuated from day to day," she wrote
with exceptional candor. And again, always blam-
ing herself far more than anyone else ever would:
"Perhaps never in my whole life have I been led
to see so distinctly the hidden iniquity and secret
evils of my heart . . . Of all persons I see myself
to be the most unfit for the place I occupy on
heathen grounds."

This was certainly an exaggeration, yet part of it
was perhaps right. However, the reasons why she
seemed sometimes to be failing in her self-appointed

task were not the ones she would ever have admitted to. After her murder by the Indians a very enlightened clergyman (who was something of an amateur psychologist in his way), wrote a wise and frank letter about Narcissa to her sister Jane. Narcissa should never, said this outspoken gentleman, have come west in the first place, for in the wilderness she had no possible outlet for her true nature. Although she longed to "redeem" the savages, she was not a missionary, in his opinion, but instead "a highly gifted, polished American lady." She belonged, he thought, not in a crude hut in the wilds among ignorant Redmen but in some more "exalted sphere." (These ideas would probably have been heartily agreed with by Dr. McLoughlin at Fort Vancouver.)

To anyone who reads Narcissa's intimate, revealing letters and journal, it becomes almost unbearable to face the great tragedy that soon befell her —the death of her only child, little gay and pretty Alice Clarissa of whom she had once written, "Oh, how many melancholy hours she has saved me, while living here alone so long, especially when her father is gone for many days together." (Thus she reveals the intense loneliness which she never directly admits.) Narcissa wrote her mother back in New York about Alice Clarissa's being able to say "Papa, Mamma, Trim, Pussy and so on." She told how, during school hours for the Indians, Alice Clarissa—a precocious little girl—would take up her own tiny stick and point out the ABC's. Once Alice came and laid her small grubby hand on a letter her mother was writing. Narcissa allowed the print to remain. It traveled all the way back across the continent as something "personal" about this little child whom Narcissa's family would never see, even in a photograph—the first white child born west of the Rocky Mountains.

For a week before Alice's death—so Narcissa wrote her family afterwards—the little girl had acted somewhat strangely. She had, for instance, insisted on sleeping in a bed of her own, not beside her mother where she had remained since her birth. Narcissa made up a pallet next to her own bed where she could reach out from time to time to touch the little girl, to cover her if need be. But although she accepted the child's odd whim she was deeply disturbed by it. She wrote, "This gave me a very strange and singular feeling that she was laid away for the grave." Yet Narcissa could also write, looking back on these curious circumstances after the tragedy had occurred, "Thus she gradually went out of my arms . . . so that I should not feel it so severely as if torn from them at once."

On the Sunday that she was drowned, Alice resisted her morning bath, an unusual occurrence on which Narcissa was also to look back with questioning pain. After family worship her father had taken her into the garden with him to look, no doubt proudly, at the fruit of his and the Indians' labors. While in the garden he gave Alice a stalk of pieplant, of which she was very fond and which she called "apple." It was his last gift to his daughter.

Alice had been playing in and out of the open door, but when it came time for dinner and she was not around, Narcissa sent Margaret, the young Indian house-helper, to get her ready for the meal. The Indian girl did not find Alice, but, without coming back to say so, went on into the garden to pick vegetables for dinner. While she was gone, Mungo, a Hawaiian servant at the mission, came into the kitchen to speak with Dr. Whitman. Mungo had to report the odd fact that he had seen two cups floating in the river. Marcus, intent on his Bible-reading, said only: "Let them be and get them out tomorrow because of the Sabbath." But Narcissa, passing to and fro in the kitchen about her household tasks, suddenly remembered her child taking two cups from the kitchen some time that morning. She cried out in terror. Where was Alice? Where was the Indian girl who had been sent to find her?

So great was Narcissa's sudden fear that everyone ran from the house at once. Reds, whites, and half-breeds gathered for the frantic search. They ran down to the brink of the river near the place where the child was actually hidden, but "as if forbidden to approach the spot, though accessible," they passed her, crossed a bend in the river far below and then back again, and then in another direction, still farther below. Some waded into the water, looking and feeling with their hands, but strangely they all entered the river below the spot where she was at last found.

Finally an old Indian entered the stream and brought out the child's body from under a root.

Narcissa, in a letter to the grandparents, re-created the full horror of that tragic moment:

"I ran to grasp her to my breast, but husband outran me and took her up from the river, and in taking her into his arms and pulling her dress from her face we thought she struggled for breath, but found afterwards that it was only the effect of the atmosphere upon her after being in the water."

Narcissa made the child's shroud herself. Some chroniclers have it that she made it from her wedding dress, but the truth seems to be that it was made from the same gray dress she wore for the long journey west. Narcissa confessed to her parents that she and Marcus kept the child for four days before the burial. "She did not begin to change in her appearance much for the first three days. This proved to be a great comfort to me, for so long as she looked natural and was so sweet and I could caress her, I could not bear to have her out of my sight." But finally she had to be put away in her grave and Narcissa took up once more the routine burden of her crowded, empty life.

Although she had no other children of her own, six years later she wrote home to say that she was now the mother of eleven: three little half-breeds— one boy and two girls—and seven orphaned emigrant children named Sager whose parents had died en route to Oregon. Of these the youngest was only five months old—a sickly, malnourished, neglected, and dirty baby whom Narcissa could not resist. "The Lord has taken our own dear child away so that we may care for the poor outcasts of the country and suffering children."

Narcissa's heart always went out to the most pitiful cases. Her little half-breed boy, whom she named David Malin after a former school friend, was brought to her in a sad condition. He was the child of an Indian woman and a wandering Spaniard. The mother abandoned him to the care of a filthy and greedy old grandmother. She in turn brought to Narcissa the three-year-old, covered with body and head lice, half-starved, with a bad burn on the foot where vicious Indians had pushed him into the fire, and a ragged bit of animal skin as his only garment.

Narcissa tried to harden her heart against him. By this time she knew the local Indians. The old grandmother would, in all likelihood, insist that Narcissa owed her something for the favor of relinquishing the unwanted child. But Narcissa's will was not strong enough to refuse the little boy a home. She was particularly upset by the way in which older Indian boys—to shame and tease him —had cut his hair. It was shaved to a strip an inch wide from ear to ear and from forehead to neck. So she took him, "washed him, oiled and bound up his wounds and dressed him and cleaned his head of lice."

David Malin soon became a favorite. As his fear of ill-treatment wore off he turned out to be a sweet, mild-mannered little lad who learned English very fast. On Sundays he would walk about the room whispering to himself: "I must not work—I must not work." Soon he, too, was singing with all Narcissa's other charges such songs as *Lord, Teach a Little Child to Pray.*

Narcissa was a good mother to her adopted brood. She was surprisingly modern. In a letter written home in 1846 she went so far as to outline her ideas for the care of children and ventured even to believe that she had made certain improvements on her mother's ways, particularly in the revolutionary matter of daily baths for children, which she reported seemed to do them no harm. The adults at Waiilatpu mission took to bathing daily in the river in summer, and at least once a week in a tub in the house the year round, and found this also beneficial.

The seven orphaned Sagers whom the Whitmans legally adopted, though without changing their names, had three happy years of life at the mission. From their memories of these years the Sager girls, whose brothers died on the dreadful day of the massacre, have left pictures of Narcissa which further reveal her temperament—half that of a firm disciplinarian, half that of a gay and gentle playmate:

"There was no danger of any of us becoming spoiled. She would point to one of us, then point to the dishes or the broom, and we would instantly get busy with our assigned tasks. She didn't scold much, but we dreaded that accusing finger pointed at us." Narcissa was very particular about regular eating and sleeping habits. The children always went to bed after a simple supper of mush and milk. There were happy picnics, however, and each child was given a little plot of land for his own garden. "Mrs. Whitman taught us the love of flowers. . . . she taught us a great deal about things of that kind and instilled in us a love of the beautiful."

Before she adopted the seven little Sagers, who, after the death of their parents, had been left to the care of other over-burdened emigrants, Narcissa had consented to bring up the half-breed daughters of Joe Meek and Jim Bridger, the mountain men. Bridger, it will be remembered, was the man on whom Marcus performed the operation for the embedded arrowhead on his first trip west, and Meek was the mountain man on whom Narcissa's young blond charm had registered so forcibly when she first came to the West. It was not easy to be responsible for these children of two worlds and it probably cost Narcissa many an anxious hour.

Eight years passed between the death of Alice Clarissa and the murder of the Whitmans.

During this period there had been increasing signs of trouble with the Indians. Neither Marcus nor Narcissa was unaware of the constant danger in which they had to live. Marcus tried his best to maintain an attitude of "Christian tolerance." He wanted to show the Indians a good example; to follow the Biblical rule of "turning the other cheek," which he once did quite literally, as he himself has described.

"He (the Indian) then took hold of my ear and pulled it and struck me on the breast ordering me to hear—as much as to say, we must let them do as they pleased. . . . When he let go I turned the other to him and he pulled that, and in this way I let him pull first one and then the other until he gave over and took my hat and threw it into the mud. I called on the Indians who were at work . . . to give it to me and I put it on my head—when he took it off again and threw it in the mud and water, of which it dipped plentifully. Once more the Indians gave it back to me and I put it on, all mud as it was, and said to him, 'Perhaps you are playing.'"

During those eight years at Waiilatpu Marcus made a famous trip alone in the winter of 1842–43 to the East Coast, through terrible weather and along unaccustomed trails. Some historians have claimed that "Whitman's Ride," as it is called, was made to "save Oregon," still in danger of being lost to Great Britain because of ignorance and indifference among people in the East and in the nation's capital. This story is not quite true, however. Marcus went east to try to persuade the Presbyterian Board—which was threatening to close the Oregon missions—to permit those missionaries already in the field to try just a little longer with the Indians. (Henry Spalding, it seemed, had been stirring up some trouble in written reports he had been sending to the Board. Yet, in spite of this fact, Marcus pleaded hard to save Henry's mission also.)

But Marcus's famous winter "ride," though it did not necessarily "save" Oregon, was very important in many other ways. He was able to spread the word "back East" that white people—especially women, even cultivated, gently-reared ones like his own wife, Narcissa—could make the western trip and set up homes in that remote outpost. Marcus visited the most famous journalist of his day, Horace Greeley, who reported him to be "the roughest looking man that we have seen this many a day." And he might well have appeared so after that long winter journey in excruciating cold, during which he had grown a four months' beard and given up all garments that were not of fur or buckskin. Even in his long hooded buffalo coat and special waterproof fur boots he had badly frozen his hands, feet and face. But Greeley was impressed enough to spread through his influential newspaper, the New York *Tribune,* what this beaten traveler had to tell him about the Promised Land far to the west.

Marcus is also thought to have gone to Washington and talked to President Tyler and the Secretary of War about the possibility of an eventually troop-patrolled Oregon Trail.

Most important of all, however, was his influence on the famous emigration of 1843. This was the first sizeable overland trek of "settlers" to the Far West. Marcus personally persuaded people to join this small stream of what was soon to become a sweeping tide of emigration. He was then able, as he turned homewards to Waiilatpu, to lend this first group his wise counsel and expert frontier experience.

While Marcus was away Narcissa had yielded to the pleas of her widely scattered "neighbors" to leave Waiilatpu temporarily. They felt that in the absence of her husband her life was no longer safe. The Cayuses had already burned down the gristmill as an act of arrogant vandalism. After one terrible night during which an Indian tried to force his way into her bedroom, Narcissa decided to go down to the village of The Dalles, on the Columbia, and spend the winter with some Methodist missionary acquaintances. She took with her her two little half-breed charges, the daughters of Joe Meek and Jim Bridger. It was the last taste of peace and comfort that poor Narcissa was ever to know.

As soon as Marcus was back, Narcissa returned to Waiilatpu although by now her health had become very bad and she feared she was losing her eyesight. Overjoyed as she was to be again with her husband, she nonetheless feared and dreaded the return. Perhaps she had premonitions of what was to come for she wrote, "I turned my face with my husband toward this dark spot, and dark indeed it seemed to be to me compared with the scenes which I had so recently been enjoying with so much zest." And again, "I felt such a dread to return to this place." She had very much hoped that her beloved sister Jane and her husband would be with Marcus when he arrived, but they had not come and we do not know why.

Although Narcissa was in bed very ill for six weeks after returning to Waiilatpu, she had finally to get up and go on with her frantically busy life. For now the westward emigrations had begun in earnest and because of the Whitmans' fame, and the strategic location of their mission, Waiilatpu became an oasis towards which many trail-weary travelers headed. It became indeed, during the first mass migrations, almost a hospital and an unofficial supply station. Marcus and Narcissa were often hard pressed to spare what these people needed, for there had been no fund supplied by a distant mission board to take care of such an unexpected and prolonged emergency as this one proved to be.

It was during this harassed time that the Sager children were driven to the Whitman door and deposited there by a kindly German doctor. He had brought the unfortunate little orphans all the way through after the tragic deaths of their father and mother on the trail. The baby of five months, who had been born beside the road and whose mother had died at her birth, would surely never have lived had it not been for Narcissa's tender care. Even Marcus, the doctor, taking one look at the little skeleton, did not feel that ailing Narcissa should assume such a responsibility, though he had voted—even before he had seen the Sager children, when word had been brought to him that they were on their way—to take all five girls and the two boys, to keep them "together as a family."

But Narcissa could not resist the sickly and neglected infant any more than she had been able to resist the poor little Indian boy, David Malin. "I felt," she wrote, "that if I must take any I wanted her as a charm to bind the rest to me. So we took her, a poor little distressed object, no larger than a babe three months old." (One of these famous Sager children was Catherine, of whom we spoke in the first chapter; the girl who had fallen under a wheel on the way west and been badly lamed. She was to be an eyewitness of the massacre that cost her foster parents and both of her brothers their lives and she wrote a vivid account of the hideous day that brought to an end all the Oregon missions.)

The western emigration of 1844 exceeded that of 1843 by about fifty percent. By 1845 the increase was three hundred percent. The Pacific Northwest was on its way to becoming American whether Congress knew or cared! And as the tide of emigration continued to stream past the Whitman door, Narcissa wrote her friends in The Dalles, farther on along the line of travelers, to "lay in a good stock of strength, patience and every needed grace" for it was, she said, like nothing so much as a "siege." Yet she also wrote home to her family that she was glad she, as a girl, had had so much experience in entertaining company. This training now helped her to keep going.

As the number of emigrants steadily increased so, inevitably, did the trouble with the Indians. It is not difficult now for us to understand how the Indians felt. The rapidly growing number of white settlers had begun to alarm them. It meant just one thing: If this white tide kept on rising, as it showed every sign of doing, what would become in time of their old easy-going way of life, of their beloved hunting and grazing grounds? The Cayuses, always more suspicious and sullen by nature than many of the other Western Indians, were quite ready to listen to the propaganda of one or two "Eastern educated" half-breeds who circulated among them telling them what was, in fact, the bitter truth—that their days as free men were numbered.

A measles epidemic was the fuse that lit the powder keg. When measles broke out among the Indians it was to them a new and fatal disease. They had no immunity to it. They treated it as they treated all illnesses, with "magic" from their medicine men and with an alternation of steam-baths and plunges into an icy river. They began to die like flies in autumn. Not even Marcus's medical knowledge could save them for, without any natural immunity in their blood, this simple childish disease took a deadly toll.

When Marcus failed to cure the Indians a rumor began to circulate that he was administering poison, not medicine. Not even the deaths of many white people from the raging measles could seem to change the Cayuses' viewpoint.

The fatal day of the twenty-ninth of November, 1847, dawned cold and foggy. It began like every other normal day among the regular mission group, grown larger now with volunteers and hired hands, swollen besides with the emigrants who had dropped down here in exhaustion after the long overland journey.

On this gray early-winter morning at the mission people were coming down with the deadly measles or slowly recovering from them, just as were the Indians in their nearby lodges. Men were at work as usual in the gristmill which had been rebuilt after its burning by the Indians. John

Sager, one of the seven emigrant children adopted by the Whitmans, was winding twine in the kitchen to be made into crude brooms. Others were studying, reading, sewing, cooking, fetching water, caring for the sick.

The school had just reopened after a brief vacation because of the measles epidemic. A tailor, then living at Waiilatpu, was making a much-needed suit of clothes for Dr. Whitman whose appearance, you will remember, Horace Greeley had found so "rough." A floor was being laid in one room. Outside some men were preparing to butcher beef.

That morning Narcissa had not appeared for breakfast. When one of the Sager girls took her meal to her room she found Narcissa weeping terribly with a handkerchief pressed against her face. In silence she motioned the girl to leave. She did not speak. She did not touch the food. Word had come at dawn that day that another child had died the night before in the lodge of the sullen Tilaukait. The doctor had already gone to perform the burial service. Did Narcissa sense then the doom that was already upon them?

It was in the afternoon that Tilaukait and Tamahas appeared at the mission house. They said they wanted some medicine. As the doctor turned away to get it they tomahawked him from behind, suddenly, savagely, without warning.

As always with first-hand accounts of shocking experiences the stories vary, but it seems likely that Marcus tried to escape. At least he managed to get outdoors. Perhaps he hoped thus to save the others from harm. After striking him several deadly, mutilating blows that he vainly tried to dodge, and after having killed John Sager who had tried to save his foster father, the two Cayuses fled.

Narcissa, who had been bathing one of the convalescent children in another part of the mission compound, rushed to her husband at the news of the assault. With the aid of two women she managed to drag Marcus indoors. She lifted him onto a settee. They all tried to stanch his heavy bleeding. But it was of no use. Though still alive, he was unconscious. There was plainly no hope for him.

Almost at once, from all sides, the Indians began to attack. One of the mission workers, who had been shot and tomahawked near the river, managed to make the house to give warning. But by the time he fell into the room where the doctor lay bleeding to death, the massacre had begun.

Narcissa went to the door to look out. Perhaps she desperately hoped to see some friendly face. She was immediately shot in the side under her left arm, and though she fell to the floor with a scream, she managed to stagger again to her feet and take charge of the terrified group that had now gathered in the room where the doctor lay. Forced to leave Marcus behind, still breathing but clearly beyond all aid, she herded everyone up the stairs to a second-story bedroom.

Hardly had they reached this room when the Indians burst in below. In the room to which the mission group had fled Narcissa found a broken gun, empty of shells. She suggested that they hold this useless gun at the head of the narrow stairwell in such a way that the Indians could not see that it was broken. By this trick they managed to keep the Indians at bay until a friendly Cayuse named Tamsucky appeared on the scene. Tamsucky told them to come down. He offered full protection and safe guidance to the nearest fort.

At first Narcissa would not believe Tamsucky. She urged him to come upstairs to speak with her in person. After some hesitation, because of the gun, Tamsucky did come up. He was then able to persuade her of his good intentions, so much so that she cried out, "God has raised us up a friend!"

It was then arranged that the adults would leave first, while the children, still promised full protection on Tamsucky's word, would remain behind for the time being. (Perhaps this was to spare them exposure in the wintry fields, since so many of them were still ill or convalescent.)

Narcissa, by now too weak from loss of blood to walk, was carried downstairs and placed on a settee. Two men from the mission group then started to carry this settee outside. But hardly had she appeared in the open than the shooting began again. Tamsucky had been a traitor!

The two men carrying Narcissa were shot at once and a number of bullets entered her body as the settee dropped to the ground. An Indian rushed up, overturned it, and thrust her down into the thick November mud. Another Indian lifted her head by its long pale golden hair and struck her face viciously with his leather quirt. No one

knows how long it took her to die. For her, however, death came sooner than for Marcus. Some of
the terrificd occupants of the mission house, still in
hiding, heard the doctor's groans far on into the
night.

Altogether fourteen people were killed at the
mission; forty-seven were taken captive and held as
hostages or made to work for the Indians.

The first outsider to reach this hideous scene was
a Catholic priest named Brouillet who, the next
day, on November 30, chanced to be visiting
Tilaukait's lodge. Father Brouillet heard there
about the massacre at Waiilatpu. He journeyed on
to the mission and helped the captive survivors
wash and bury the dead who were still lying in
the open in all their ghastly mutilation. He then
read a burial service over them with quaking
knees, while the Cayuses stood looking on at a little distance, painted and armed.

It was this same priest who probably saved the
life of Henry Spalding. Traveling away from the
mission, Father Brouillet came on Spalding riding
towards it to see his little daughter, Eliza, who was
spending some time at the Whitman school. The
priest urged Henry to return with all speed to the
unhostile Nez Perces. He told him that his
daughter's life had been spared. (Actually Eliza,
though only ten years old, had helped the priest
sew the bodies of the dead into sheets for burial.)

Henry, in fear and horror, did return at once
to his mission at Lapwai to warn Eliza and the

friendly Nez Perces. He then rode back with all speed to Waiilatpu, still uncertain of his daughter's fate. He found Eliza quite safe. She had by now been pressed into service as an interpreter between the Indians and the other occupants of the mission who were still held as hostages.

At Waiilatpu Henry sat down and wrote back to New York State a full, detailed and horrible description of the last days of the Prentiss's beloved daughter, Narcissa—a letter which has survived the years. Perhaps Henry felt that it was better to describe the tragedy fully rather than to gloss it over. Surely as he wrote he must have regretted the difficulties he had sometimes made for the Whitmans, the criticisms of Narcissa which he had not been able to keep from expressing.

Down in the valley of the Willamette angry settlers got together a force of fifty riflemen and sent them out after the murderous Cayuses. Hearing that the riflemen were on their way, the Cayuses, after first looting the mission, fled into the mountains. For two years they wandered, desperate and homeless, until at last five of them, including the known murderers, gave themselves up to justice.

The riflemen helped the released captives at the Whitman mission pack up whatever was left of their meagre belongings and set off down the Columbia River by boat, under the guardian wing of the mighty Hudson's Bay Company—a force all the Western Indians respected. Only one person from the mission did not go—little David Malin.

He was left behind on the river bank. It is hard to believe such cruelty. Narcissa, his kind foster mother, was dead. In thcir state of shock and loss, there was no one among the survivors who felt like taking responsibility for him. Perhaps they feared his Indian blood. Even Henry Spalding did not save him. Abandoned for the second time in his life, the little Indian boy, alone in a driving rain, passes from history "crying as though his heart were breaking."

Joe Meek, the mountain man who had so much admired beautiful Narcissa when he first saw her riding westward, then began to "make history" himself. Meek was one of the riflemen sent by the Willamette Valley settlers to the site of the Whitman tragedy. His own daughter's body was among those he had to help remove from the first shallow collective grave and bury more deeply. (Wolves had already been making grisly meals off the remains of the corpses.) Soon after Meek left the scene of the tragedy at Waiilatpu, he set off alone for the nation's capital on the far side of a snowbound continent. He was going, as a one-man embassy from Oregon, to plead with his cousin, President James K. Polk, for government protection for the Far Western settlers and for the admission of Oregon as a Territory.

The massacre of the Whitmans, made public through Meek's mission to Washington, horrified all who heard of it. Actually Narcissa's family, and Marcus's also, first learned of the terrible fate that had befallen them by reading the story Meek had given to the newspapers of Washington; an account picked up and reprinted by almost every Eastern paper. (Henry's detailed letter about the tragedy arrived much later.)

President Polk was fired by his long-lost cousin's vivid story of the massacre and his report on the beauties and value of the Far Western lands. He determined to acquire this part of the West for the Union. On the very last day before Polk's term as President expired Oregon was officially proclaimed a Territory. This was in 1848, forty-two years after Lewis and Clark and Sacajawea returned from their transcontinental explorations.

Thus the martyrdom of Narcissa and Marcus Whitman beyond all doubt helped decide the fate of this portion of the American West.

Today historical museums treasure not only Narcissa's remarkable letters and journal, along with other documents from early mission days, but even locks of her bright hair, cut from the mangled body that poor Joe Meek had to help rebury in Waiilatpu ground.

The mission precincts have been made a national monument under the supervision of the National Park Service. The site of the ruins has been carefully excavated and plainly marked for all to see, and there is a small museum to house artifacts excavated from the site. Every year thousands of visitors come out from Walla Walla to climb the hill of the rye grass and gaze down at the shaft that marks the grave of the victims of that fateful November day in 1847. Perhaps they wonder, as they stand there in the clear bright light, where on the green plains below lie the bones of little Alice Clarissa Whitman, that "treasure invaluable" who briefly gladdened the daily cares and the lonely hours of the first white woman to cross the Rocky Mountains.

CHAPTER FOUR

EIGHT ON HER HONEYMOON

$\mathcal{T}$HE HONOR of being the third white woman to cross the Rocky Mountains is generally credited to Mary Richardson Walker from the state of Maine.

Like the two women who preceded her, Narcissa Whitman and Eliza Spalding, Mary went west as a missionary to the Indians in the year 1837. She traveled mostly by horseback all the way from Maine to a place near Spokane in the present state of Washington, crossing the plains in a party of eight honeymooners.

These four honeymooning couples were, like Mary and her husband, Elkanah, bound on the same high adventure—that of bringing Christianity to the Indians west of the Rocky Mountains.

There is no record that Mary actually crossed the Continental Divide first among the women of this particular party. It just seems likely, to all those who have read her lively and entertaining diaries. Her boundless interest in everything around her, her curiosity, courage, and zest for life would have led her, one feels, to spur her horse first over the invisible line that marked what was then known as "the backbone of America."

It is safe to say, however, that Mary would never have been the first over the Divide if her bridegroom Elkanah had not been riding behind with the "cow column" instead of up front with the guides where she was. Elkanah had very strict views about how a "lady" and a "missionary's wife" should conduct herself. He also believed in "men first," as most men did. The differences of viewpoint between Mary and "Mr. W.," as she often called him, make for some amusing and touching reading in her detailed journals of the trip west and their life together in the wilderness.

Mary's remarkable personal journals were written first for her eye alone. She began to keep them as a girl in Maine. After her marriage, when the Walkers went to the Far West, Elkanah chanced to read a few entries. It has been suggested that Mary hoped he would take a peek since she had written down a few remarks about her seeming inability to please him. In any case, this glimpse of her journal seemed to help Elkanah to mend his critical ways.

Long after Mary and Elkanah as husband and wife had found peace and a good relationship together, and long after they were both in their graves, some of Mary's descendants decided to let interested strangers read and enjoy their ancestor's account of life in those stirring days when the War

Department was required to issue passports for anyone crossing America.

Thus it is that Mary Walker's journals, kept so faithfully in the midst of a life of constant toil, hardship and danger, became a most valuable public record of life in the Far West as lived by one unusual woman.

Mary's story begins in East Baldwin, Maine. Her diary tells us that she was only nine years old when she first decided that she wanted to "go to the heathen as a missionary." She never lost sight of this early dream. Perhaps, like Narcissa Whitman, part of her desire to be a missionary sprang from a wish to see more of the world than the village where she was born.

Mary was always a student. She read everything on which she could lay her hands. When she went away to college at Maine Wesleyan, a great piece of good fortune for a girl of her day, she made an exceptional record for herself. Anxious to know how her work compared with the men students, she at last got up courage enough to put the question to one of her professors. He replied, "Better, much better." He then added, "Aren't you ashamed of yourself, Mary?" For girls in the early nineteenth century were not supposed to compete with boys in brains. It was unfitting and even a little brazen!

In those days women like Mary were often called "bluestockings," a term that went back to the eighteenth century in London when women who were the first "feminists" and "intellectuals" had refused to wear conventional clothes.

In her early twenties Mary tried to go abroad as a missionary. She went around among friends, neighbors and former teachers getting testimonials as to her character and conduct. She even wrote a recommendation for herself in which she said quite frankly that she was "perfectly at home in the school room, nursery, kitchen or wash room or employed with the needle." She did admit to the charge of having an "aspiring mind" (definitely rather dangerous) but added that she strove to "cultivate a spirit of humility; to be willing to do something and be nothing if duty required."

Mary hoped for a post as a teacher in faraway Siam. But again, like Narcissa Whitman before her, she was to discover that "single females" were not acceptable to the American mission boards. Had she been allowed to go to Bangkok, she might have given us some accounts of the ways of Siamese royalty quite as lively as those of *Anna and the King of Siam.*

Again, as in Narcissa's case—and also in answer to direct prayers for a "pious husband"—along came a man to make missionary life possible for her. A match-making friend, interested in Mary's wish to be a missionary-teacher, presented Elkanah Walker, who had a similar ambition. Mary was very interested but she did have some qualms, for she was being pursued by a much more "suitable catch," a mysterious neighbor named "G."

The mysterious "G" of Mary's journal was unlike Elkanah in many ways. He was, Mary admitted, "rich and brilliant." Elkanah was not. But "G" was satisfied with life on a Maine farm. El-

kanah looked toward a farther horizon. Mary too
hoped for a wider use for her boundless energies
and inquiring mind than life as a farmer's wife,
no matter how comfortably "fixed."

Not everyone in Mary's circle thought much of
Elkanah Walker, tall, thin, gangling and very shy
(except on paper where he was able to express
quite warm sentiments to Mary). Although Mary's
sisters found him rather engaging, her brothers—
whenever Elkanah appeared—made Mary miserable
by imitating the hoarse cries and gawky movements
of a young crane they had recently captured.

But Mary knew real worth when she saw it. She
began by respecting and admiring this good but
very moody man. They went through some trying
times of "adjustment" because of the differences in
their temperaments and the trials of the primitive
life they undertook together. They ended by loving
one another dearly, as Mary's journals clearly show,
in spite of Mary's early warnings in courtship days
that she did hope he would remember she intended
"always to retain her personal identity." In other
words, she would remain herself, no matter how
much he might wish to change her!

The Walkers had expected after their marriage to
be sent as missionaries to Zululand in Africa. However, some Zulu chiefs started fighting one another
with such vigor that the Mission Board decided to
send the Walkers to the Far West instead.

Not that the risks of going to Oregon were any
less great than a trip to Zululand. Even Mary,
who didn't hesitate a moment about "foreign

travel," who indeed welcomed it, referred to this part of the American Continent as "the riddlings of Creation." She had undoubtedly read typical statements of the times like this example: "The whole country is the most irreclaimable barren waste known to mankind except the desert of Sahara. As to healthfulness, the ravages of malaria defy all history to furnish a parallel."

Some of the Maine neighbors thought it showed more bravado than courage to set off across the great "dry sea" and over the snow-crowned Rockies to still unclaimed Indian lands near the Pacific Ocean. "Now isn't that just like Mary Richardson to go galloping off across the plains on a wild buffalo!" remarked one of them with a sniff. Perhaps this was the same neighbor whom Mary had once greatly shocked by sitting down on the floor in front of the fire on a hearth rug—something no proper "lady" would ever have dreamed of doing. Mary must often have laughed at this memory after she got to the Far West and had to live for months without so much as a floor to walk on, much less to sit on!

One of the things that makes Mary Walker's trip west and her life in the wilderness so meaningful to us, reading about it a hundred years later, is the observant eye she bent on everything she saw. So anxious was she to make the most of her great adventure that we find her in Cincinnati before the journey has more than just begun, pleading for the purchase of certain books. They were big books, hard to carry across the plains when every item had to be so carefully weighed and considered, taken or discarded on the grounds of "necessity."

One of the books Mary wanted was about plants. One was about stones and rocks. One was about minerals. Not only did she want them, she considered them a "necessity." The problem of how to feed her mind in wilderness solitude seemed more important than how to feed her body.

The idea of the importance of a basic library on stones, plants and minerals didn't appeal to everyone of the missionary group. Not even to Elkanah. But Mary wheedled and begged, and no doubt argued too in her logical way, and finally she notes triumphantly in her journal: "Think I shall prevail at last in having a botany, geology and mineralogy."

Mary began to make good use of these books on the long journey west.

As she rode day after weary day across the endless plains, up the slopes of hills and mountains, through the streams and rivers, we find her writing with satisfaction, "How much the time is shortened by the company of plants and minerals." This enthusiasm was unhappily not shared by her bridegroom. We find Mary also writing, "I wish Mr. W. would feel as much interest in viewing the works of nature as I do. I think the journey would be much less wearisome for him."

To Mary, with her ever-observant eye, no day could ever be really dull or boring. She was always looking at the land, not just riding through it. "Passed some granite," she would note. "Haven't seen any for a long time." Or, "Volcanic rock on either side. Some basalt." Once when they stopped at some mineral springs, curious Mary dismounted in order to sample the surrounding soil; soft, white, unfamiliar. "It tasted like slacked lime," she wrote. Once on a day when her horse had "tumbled" her over his head, she still found the spirit to experiment at biscuit making with water from a natural soda spring at which they had camped for the night. According to Mary the water tasted like "good spruce beer. . . . I made biscuits with it as good and light as if I had used the nicest yeast and let the dough rise just enough. Used nothing but the water and a little salt and baked them as soon as mixed." So she lets her mother back home in Maine know about domestic details of caravan life.

Mary was fascinated by the part of the American land that has been formed into fantastic shapes by the fires, floods and upheavals of prehistoric times. "The bluffs resemble statuary," she wrote excitedly, "castles, forts . . . as if Nature, tired of waiting the advance of civilization, has erected her own temples."

One of the great landmarks of the "dry sea," populated then only by herds of buffalo, was the immense monolith called Independence Rock. This rock was to become, in the years of the great westward migrations, a sort of registry of passing travelers who, pausing here to camp, carved their names and dates on its towering sides. Mary did not carve her name on Independence Rock but she did chip a piece from it for her rock collection.

The piece she chipped has been preserved in the Oregon Historical Museum in Portland along with the worn side-saddle in which she rode so many thousands of miles.

Although she was usually calm, efficient and good-humored, Mary had her black moments too. Like all westward-moving people who came from good homes, particularly the women, she had spells of wondering about her ability to endure the privations of wilderness life. Crossing the plains was far from easy for anyone. Tempers often wore thin, particularly after days of bad weather. "Obliged to sleep in our blankets, wet as when taken from our horses," wrote Mrs. Eells who was later to be

Mary's neighbor at Tshimakain. Mary herself noted, "Our bed was utterly flooded."

During one prolonged rainy spell Mary was discovered by the Reverend Eells having what she always referred to as "a good bawl." Mr. Eells had never seen Mary in tears. He had described her as "strong and cheery . . . a farmer's daughter—a country cultured lady." But now he found her seated on her piled-up bedding in the Walker tent, sobbing bitterly. Astonished to find her in such a state, he asked what the matter was (though it must have been pretty plain!). Mary replied through her tears, "I am just thinking how comfortable my father's hogs are."

Just like the Whitmans before them, the Walkers and the other missionaries of their group had journeyed west with a fur caravan from St. Louis. When after weeks of travel they finally reached the "place of rendez-vous" in the Rockies, they barely escaped disaster. A mistake had been made in the location of the spot where the trappers and the St. Louis traders were to meet to exchange their furs and supplies. The eight honeymooners feared for a while that they had lost their next set of guides, the men who were going to take them on farther west.

Fortunately, however, someone had scrawled a message on the wall of an empty mountain cabin that "white women" could be seen at such and such a place. This incredible news brought along the missing guides in a hurry!

Looking at the relative spaces on a map, it would seem that once having reached the rendez-vous for trappers and traders in the Rocky Mountains, the journey for the Walkers was nearly over. Actually, however, the greatest dangers still lay before them. The perils of mountain horseback riding were by no means insignificant, particularly for a pregnant woman, which Mary now was.

"You know I am not skittish at all," she wrote home after a descent "steeper than the roof of a building commonly is . . . but I could scarcely sit my horse." During those days of hard mountain riding, Elkanah lost his wedding coat, a loss so sorrowful that Mary underlined it in her journal. He also gave his watch such a severe jolting that she was sure it would have to go to England for repairs. (To be gone at least a year!) The ladies all lost their veils—a notation that gives us a picture of their attempts, in the high altitude, to protect themselves against the ravages of insects and the burning sun.

At last there came the happy day when the little company of weary travelers rode into the Whitman mission yard at Waiilatpu, there to be warmly welcomed by Marcus and Narcissa. And now at last a few of their worst trials seemed behind them. At least, for the present, they need no longer sleep with a musket beside them at nights. It seemed "good" not to have to, was Mary's only comment.

There were by no means, however, real conveniences or comforts for the newcomers at the small crowded quarters of the Whitmans. Mary, waiting for her first-born child, had only a small unheated room to herself. She wrote home that she dreaded the coming of cold weather when she would have to crowd into the one room that had a stove in it. How she would have loved to get some letters just then! But the Whitmans themselves hadn't yet heard from home after almost two years' absence.

Elkanah went off on a scouting trip, looking for the site of their future mission. Mary envied him his freedom of movement. She began soon to have her first unpleasant experiences with the inquisitive Indians. She seemed never safe from their prying eyes. They had a disconcerting way of appearing suddenly—always without making any noise to announce themselves—in the doorway, at the window, inside the very room in which the white strangers were sitting. There they would stand, gazing in mockery or wonderment, or following like a shadow which would never be lost—ill-smelling, lice-ridden, flea-bearing.

Later from their own cabin Mary was to write in brief despair, "I scarcely do anything from morning till night without being seen by some of them. Sometimes I feel . . . I cannot endure it any longer and then I think if I do not teach them in this way, I never shall in any way. [Yet] I suspect that many of them never think of trying to imitate the things they see me do any more than we should think of imitating a play actor whom we had been witnessing."

Mary, who had remained at the Whitman mission in order to have Dr. Whitman's help at the time of her child's delivery, was very glad to leave when her boy, Cyrus, was born. She was anxious for a place of her own, though it was only to be a fourteen-foot-square log hut with a grass-and-dirt roof leaking mud in every rain, a dirt floor with pine needles strewn on it, and the skins of animals tacked at windows and doors.

The Walkers and the Eells had chosen to settle together among the Spokane Indians (also known as Flatheads because of a way they had of deforming their babies' skulls in infancy). Their mission cabins were built in an idyllic little valley called Tshimakain, named by the Indians for a spring that bubbled there.

Mary has left a description of this untouched country-side which was to be her home for nine years and, perhaps in a sense, forever her "spirit-

ual" home. Her words describe an unawakened
land where few human beings have ever set foot.

> This is a beautiful country,
> Still a kind of gloom seems to pervade it
> As if Nature were asleep,
> Or rather the face of the ground.
> The whole country might be supposed to be
> Enjoying a long Sabbath.

Cyrus was the first of seven Walker children. At
the births of some of these babies Mary had only
nervous Elkanah's help. Some of them came into
the world with Dr. Whitman standing by, having
ridden all the way from his mission to deliver the
new little Walker.

But the doctor didn't always make it on time.
Once Mary met him at the door with her newborn child in her arms.

Her journal lets us know something of her
strength and simple courage on the days of her
seven children's births:

"Rested well last night; awoke about four A.M.
Rose at five, helped about milking, but by the
time I had done that, found it necessary to call
my husband and soon the Dr. Had scarcely time
to dress and comb my hair. Before eight was delivered of a fine daughter."

And again:

"Rose about five. Had early breakfast. Got my
house work done about nine. Baked six loaves of
bread. Made a kettle of mush and have now a
suet pudding and beef boiling. My girl (Indian)
has ironed and I have managed to put my clothes

away and set my house in order. May the merciful
be with me through the unexpected scene. Nine
o'clock P.M. was delivered of another son."

Even when her little flock was beginning to
spring up around her skirts in mushroom style,
Mary faithfully made entries in her journal. We
see from these pages how, in spite of the drudgery
of her life, she found time for the little extras that
give a child pleasure. Once she wrote about sitting
up late to make a "rag baby" for little Abigail
and then not being able to resist going to the
child's bed and waking her just to see her look of
utter joy.

Though there were long days of solitude for
Mary in the lonely countryside, there was, always,
endless work to be done. Just to read the chores
enumerated in her wilderness journal makes the
back ache.

Her work day averaged sixteen hours. Sixteen
hours of washing, ironing, sewing, mending, painting, carpentering, baking, repairing roofs and chimneys, helping the invalid Mrs. Eells ("cleaned Mrs.
E's earthen ware. Cooked for both families"), milking six cows night and morning, making soap and
butter and cheese.

Mary was accustomed to sit up late, either work-
ing or reading, and she usually rose before others.
Her energy was tireless! Her lively mind allowed
her no rest. Although, in order to help her husband with his work among the Indians, she set out
to learn the Spokane language, she frequently
chided herself for making so little progress in the

translation of hymns into the Indian tongue. This was a difficult task, as the sounds the Spokanes made in speech were like nothing so much as "the sounds of husking corn."

Mary had to teach the Indians white ways by constant precept and example. She also tried to give them some knowledge of the great world outside their small compass of experience. She set out to teach them geography with the aid of eggshells painted to represent the globe.

She continued also to make good use of that little library she bought in Cincinnati. When, as a joyful interruption to her months of solitude, men of learning came to the hidden green valley of Tshimakain, she had something to share with them besides domestic chitchat. Indeed, when there were fresh minds to tap, she was so impatient with time-wasting trivia that she once commented tartly on the Reverend Eells's monopoly of the conversation. (This was during the great Peter Skene Ogden's visit to Tshimakain.)

"We had a very pleasant visit, except there was too much trifling conversation and Bro. E's ego was quite prominent. When a man of such extensive information is present, I regret to have the time occupied with trifles."

Perhaps Mary was not at all sorry that both husbands chanced to be away when members of the famous Wilkes Expedition came to spend the night. This expedition was surveying the unclaimed West for a still somewhat indifferent United States government. Mary, always the learner, was happy to "sit at the feet" of these distinguished men, all of them experts in fields where she was a solitary but eager amateur: botany, natural history, taxidermy, mineralogy, philology. She could show them many specimens of plants and rocks and stuffed animals, all of her own collecting. For a few hours at least she enjoyed the kind of conversation that her soul so often craved.

On the occasion of the visit of the Wilkes' party, it also fell to Mary to bargain with the Indian chief for some horses the men of the expedition badly needed. Thanks to her eloquence, and due to her patient study of the difficult Indian language, she was able to obtain "three of the chief's best horses" for which he in turn received "nine blankets and one shirt."

After the white men had gone Mary wrote in her journal that the "chief complimented me very highly for my eloquence. Said I talked as forcefully as Mr. W. or Mr. E. would have done. That the gentlemen would not have gotten the horses but for me." For an Indian accustomed to the subservience of his women this was indeed a compliment.

Word of the remarkable white woman in the wilderness near Spokane spread among other travelers to the West.

Mary's joy in her all too infrequent contact with learned men appears in a number of journal entries. Of two visiting botanists she wrote, "Had a pleasant time as I found they knew much more than I on the subject." Again, spurred on by visitors, "Spent most of the day arranging dried plants. Find my collection is becoming large." Of a visiting mineralogist, "He took a specimen of the soda and several minerals that I happened to have." One diary entry about the painter Paul Kane (who was unknowingly to paint, while visiting at Waiilatpu, portraits of the two Indians who were later to murder the Whitmans) remarks in a wry way, "an ungodly man of not much learning but he gave me considerable information about birds."

Like a modern hostess Mary kept a guest book and autograph album in her primitive cabin. In it a number of early Western explorers and travelers wrote warm sentiments about Mary and her amazing fund of information. They also expressed gratitude for the "touch of home" they had come upon in her cabin in the wilds.

This autograph book of Mary's dated back to her former life in Maine. On the day of her wedding to Elkanah, Mary's mother had written in it some verses of "advice." Mary must have often had occasion to turn to these entries at times when Elkanah was particularly critical or low in mind due to his almost chronic state of indigestion. Among her mother's selections were these two lines of verse:

> *Think not, the husband gained, that all is done.*
> *The prize of happiness must still be won.*

And so, visitors gone, brief excitement over, we find Mary writing in her diary, "I felt very lonely after they left." But then, determined on that "prize of happiness" that depended so much on her own attitude, she would again take up cheerfully the duties of her hard life, including even midwifery to Mrs. Eells and the kind of "doctoring" to a sick husband that often has a very strange ring to modern ears:

"Mr. W. sick with a sore throat. Took nitre and Ipecac, put pepper and vinegar on the outside; applied a hot rock to the throat and feet at night, got easier."

Mary also made all the family's garments and their shoes: "Cut out eight pairs of shoes." She salted beef, cleaned tripe, wove carpets. churned, tried tallow, dipped candles, "sat up all night . . . dipped twenty-four dozen." And all this labor was accomplished without even the primitive equipment that then passed for "conveniences" among more favored American women. Yet, after she had been living for some time with that rough dirt floor, she is able to write cheerily, "Find it pleasant to have a floor to wash again."

But "Sometimes I wish there was a way to live easier," she could also admit, just as she would also remind herself that she had not traveled 3,000 miles only to be a household drudge. "Is this kind of labor all a missionary has to do?" she would ask herself when chimneys fell down, frost killed the first vines, Mr. Eells' house caught fire, Mrs. Eells took sick again, a high wind came up just as she was picking over feathers for a mattress, horses strayed from the pasture, cows too, and the babies were specially "tendful." All this with Mr. W. somewhere in the trackless wilds, overdue home by hours or even days.

Although it is unusual for Mary really to break down and complain, when she does so she is often at her most entertaining.

"Felt quite out of patience this morning on account of the miserable old door and the cats and the Indians; first one and then another would knock out a piece and the wind came in without the least ceremony, so that I could not be comfortable in the room long enough to get my breakfast. I was tempted to fret, but concluded I would go to work and see if I could not fix it. I nailed it together as well as I could and then lined it with mats so that it is quite comfortable and tonight the weather is more moderate."

No matter how tired she was, or how irksome and unending her work hours, Mary still had simple but sure ways of enjoying life and cheering herself up. Nature unfolded to her an ever-fascinating series of pictures. ". . . A rainbow about three P.M. such as I never saw before," and she describes it in detail for her own pleasure. Or, "About six the sun shone out and we observed a big bird of the hawk or eagle kind, on the tip top of a tree a short distance from the house, drying himself in the sun." She watched him for twenty minutes and then, wanting a closer look, went to the foot of the tree at which he took fright and flew off.

Perhaps the most touching and unconsciously humorous section in Mary's diary is her account of her experiences in stuffing dead birds, fish and animals bought from the Indians, an occupation that fills a number of entries in the year 1847:

"August 1847 Tues. Purchased a bow and a trout and salmon skin and spent half the afternoon stuffing and fixing them.

"Wed 4. Bought a mocking bird.

"Thurs 5. Stuffed a sparrow skin and bought a rattlesnake skin ready stuffed, except that it wanted fixing a little nicer. . . .

"Fri 6. Purchased a duck skin and stuffed it,

also a cross bill. Mr. W. gets out of sorts not liking my new trade of stuffing birds, etc.

"Tues 10. Purchased a few stuffed skins but think I will wait until I can procure arsenic before I collect more.

"Wed 18. Bought four partridges.

"Sat 21. In the afternoon skinned and stuffed a small bird.

"Wed 25. Spent the afternoon in skinning a crane; think I will not undertake another crane soon."

Although other diary entries clearly indicate that Elkanah did not share this particular interest of Mary's, he did at least allow her to proceed. "Got permission to continue collecting objects in natural history," she writes. For once we feel that Elkanah may have been, at times, a sorely tried man. He must have found it difficult to understand why a woman surrounded on every side by wild life should persist in her effort to bring it dead into her crowded cabin. Perhaps, however, this was Mary's way of establishing a subtle dominance over the all-powerful world of nature on which human beings had here made so little impression.

It was one of Mary's favorite visitors, John Mix Stanley, a painter like Paul Kane, also studying Indian life in the Far West, who sent back to his recent hosts the terrible news that was forever to alter the course of the Walkers' lives.

Stanley had been staying with the Walkers for some days. Mary liked this artist much better than Paul Kane who had also recently visited at Tshimakain and had gone on to the Whitman mission. Stanley, although he specialized in Indian portraits, made a "likeness" of Elkanah while he was the Walkers' guest and one of little Abigail as well. (These are among five pictures that survived a great fire at the Smithsonian in 1865 which tragically destroyed all Stanley's life work.)

When Stanley left the Walkers' they sent with him, as guide and companion, a faithful Spokane Indian named Solomon. Solomon was to conduct Stanley to the Whitman mission and while there would notify the doctor that Mary was expecting her sixth child very soon.

On their way to Waiilatpu, Solomon and Stanley met an Indian woman and a child who told them of the massacre of the Whitmans and warned them that they should not go on. They should proceed instead to the nearby fort at Walla Walla.

Solomon and Stanley set out for the fort in all haste. On their way they met another Indian. He told them the same terrible story. This Indian, however, carried a gun and he asked Stanley if he was "an American." Stanley very cleverly told the Redman that he was a "Buckeye" which meant simply that he came from the state of Ohio. The Indian didn't know what a "Buckeye" was and he let Stanley pass.

As soon as faithful Solomon had delivered Stanley safely to the fort, he hurried back to Tshimakain with a letter the artist wrote to Mary and Elkanah.

Elkanah opened the letter in the midst of his family and the Eells who had gathered to hear the latest news from the Whitmans. When Elkanah broke the seal and scanned the first lines, he turned deathly white and could hardly speak. Then in a voice trembling with horror, he read the terrible details: "how Dr. and Mrs. Whitman, Mr. Rodgers, another member of the mission, the two Sager boys, their [the Whitmans'] adopted sons, and many other men had been killed by the Cayuse Indians, and that the women and children had been taken prisoners."

There had been, before this terrible moment, some talk among the two missionary families at Tshimakain about the Cayuses' changed attitude towards the Whitmans at Waiilatpu. No one, however, had believed that such a brutal murder could possibly take place. To Mary, soon to bear a child, the news came as such a shock that she hardly wrote a word about it in her journal.

The Walkers and the Eells realized at once that their own lives and the lives of their little children were now in the hands of the Spokanes, among whom they had dwelt peaceably for nine years. What if the friendly Spokanes were suddenly to become killers like the Cayuses? Sometimes Indian troubles spread like an infection. The white people were helpless. There was nothing to do but pray.

The Spokanes tried to reassure the worried Eells and Walkers about their unfailing loyalty. Mary wrote in her journal a few days later, "The Indians say they [the neighboring Cayuses] must kill them first before they can us."

Whether she took heart from this promise or not, it is clear that she was able somehow to go on about her daily life much as usual: sewing, cooking, taking care of her own sick children and sick Indians, all down with the same raging measles that had brought on the Whitman tragedy.

Christmas came and went but no one had any heart for a celebration. On the last day of the year 1847, another son was born to Mary. Since Dr. Whitman was dead, she bore the child alone.

Mary named the new boy after a favorite brother. As she did so she must have thought with longing of the peace that would have been hers had the baby arrived back home in Maine instead of here in wild Oregon among Indians on the war-path.

The Oregon mission of the American Board came to an end when the Whitmans were massacred. After this dark event it was only a matter of time until the Walkers and the Eells were forced to leave the home they had come to love in the little green valley of the bubbling spring.

Around the New Year, they received a terrifying warning letter from Henry Spalding. It served to increase their fears. Henry advised them, as they valued their lives, to leave with their children just as soon as possible.

The Walkers and the Eells decided to talk it over once more with their Indians, who were still swearing loyalty and protection. The old chief of the Spokanes was very upset at their thought of leaving. He told the missionaries that if they left, all the other white people of the sparsely settled pioneer countryside, as well as other peaceable In-

dian tribes, would make a laughingstock of the
Spokanes and say they "could not protect their
teachers." (Among all the Western Indians the
Spokanes were said to be specially sensitive to
ridicule.)

So shaken were the Walkers by the old chief's
moving pleas that they decided, in spite of Spalding's dire warnings, to wait a little longer. Elkanah
went to Fort Colville to talk over their decision
with the authorities there.

The day after he left, Mary wrote in her diary:
"A lonely anxious day. Our way is so dark and I
feel so uncertain what duty is. It seems almost as
bad as death to think of leaving here."

Yet leave they finally did, trying to tell themselves—as their hearts were breaking—that it would
not be forever, just until the Indian troubles died
down. But Mary noted in her journal on that sad
March day when they finally turned their backs on
the green valley of Tshimakain, "We left home
about noon, perhaps to return no more." The
very quietness of her words reveals how deep her
feelings were. She had no heart to write more.

The little group of homeless people now set out
on a slow journey that was to carry them down
into the peaceful valley of the Willamette—already
more settled and protected than other western communities.

On their way, the little caravan of men, women,
children and soldiers passed the ruined and deserted mission of the Whitmans. One of the young
Walkers saw his mother pick up a bit of the golden
hair of Narcissa and show it to Mrs. Eells. Here

again Mary was too much overcome to write anything at all in her diary—though she must have had thoughts, many thoughts, of the day she arrived, heavy with child, and was helped from her horse in the yard before the kitchen door of this other brave, now martyred, woman.

But Elkanah wrote something about their brief shocked pause at the Whitman mission: "The fields were all grown up to weeds, their fences broken down. The bones and hair of the Missionary and his wife, with others, had been scattered over the plains by the wolves . . . I will not attempt to describe my feelings." Nor could he speak of Mary's, but one remark conveys a great deal about normally cheerful, strong Mary in those dark hours: "Mrs. Walker is much cast down, more so than I have ever seen her before."

Yet it seems likely that Mary rallied before the trip was out. An officer among the soldiers who were guarding them had written of her just four days before they came upon the sad remains of Waiilatpu:

"Passed the day quite agreeably in the company of Madam Walker, conversing on the natural history of the region, character of the natives, their manners and customs." They had also talked at length, he reported, about the kinds of geologic formations through which they passed. The officer concluded his remarks about his traveling companion by saying, "An intelligent and virtuous woman, her price is far about rubies."

Mary was anxious that her children should never forget the lovely valley of their birth, their early

childhood among Indians, their log-house home, or
the log chapel where the Spokanes gathered in
blankets and robes to follow the white man's style
of worship. She wrote a descriptive verse about it
for each of them to keep. It reads the way an old
sampler looks.

Tshimakain! Oh, how fine, fruits and flowers abounding,
And the breeze, through the trees, life and health con-
ferring.

And the rill, near the hill, with its sparkling water
Lowing herds and prancing steed round it used to
  gather.
And the Sabbath was so quiet and the log house chapel
Where the Indians used to gather in their robes and
  blankets.
Now it stands, alas! forsaken: no one with the Bible
Comes to teach the tawny skailu* of Kai-kó-len-só-tin.†
Other spots on earth may be to other hearts as dear;
But not to me; the reason why, it was the place that
  bore me.

After Mary took up life in a small pioneer community, she was not so faithful with her journal
entries. We don't know why. Was there less that
interested her? Fewer strange animals, birds, flowers,
Indians—even fewer intelligent visitors?

The slow tempo of her days was quickened once
by a trip back to Maine on the first transcontinental railroad. In the state of her birth, not so greatly
changed since she left it, Mary was pointed out as
a curiosity—the first local woman to ride across the
great western plains and over the distant Rockies.
Perhaps, even, the buffalo myth had gathered
weight with the passing of the years.

But Mary returned to Oregon from Maine. The
Far West had now become her "home."

She spent most of the rest of her life on an
Oregon farm, accepting bravely the very fate that
she had wished to avoid in Maine so many years
before. As for Elkanah, he became a wandering
preacher. Mary survived him by twenty years.

* *Skailu*—people.   † *Kai-kó-len-só-tin*—God.

The story is told that as an old woman Mary would sometimes get down her worn sidesaddle, place it on a rocking chair, wrap around her the long cloak she had worn across the plains, and thus sit by the hour, dreamily rocking, gazing into empty space. Was she seeing again in all their untouched freshness and beauty the green valleys, the far-stretching plains, the great rocks carved by weather and time, the distant snow-capped Shining Mountains of her young woman's journey across an untraveled continent? Was she remembering again, as in a dimming happy dream, how she was forever dismounting from her horse, to her bridegroom's occasional annoyance, to pick new flowers, study a rare plant, collect strange rocks as the little band of eight missionary honeymooners moved steadily westward, day after slow day, in the direction of the setting sun?

CHAPTER FIVE

ONE DARE NOT BE NERVOUS IN OREGON

ONE MUST not be nervous in Oregon!" So wrote Sister Mary Loyola on the fourteenth of October in 1845 from the mission house of St. Paul on the lonely banks of a far western river called the Willamette. She was penning a letter in her neat convent-trained hand to her Mother Superior far away in Belgium, in the old cobbled and gabled town of Namur.

An Indian runner had just come with the news that an English vessel would be sailing for Europe from the mouth of the nearby Columbia River in a few days' time. Any letter that Sister Loyola or one of her five companion nuns would send back to Fort Vancouver by the Indian courier would, with good sailing luck, reach Belgium about seven months hence.

So Loyola was hastening to prepare another packet of news about life in the wilderness for the Reverend Mother of the secluded ivy-hung convent the six nuns had left forever almost two years before.

Loyola went on to explain why giving way to nerves in the remote Oregon wilderness was plainly impossible. "It is not uncommon," she wrote, "to see wolves and mountain lions in broad daylight. As to snakes, we meet them often, even in the vegetable garden among our melons and cucumbers. . . . We kill snakes and chase wild cattle as you would brush aside a fly. Only this morning we had to drive out eight wild horses."

Sister Loyola was not boasting. She went on to say that they had, indeed, grown quite accustomed to all these unusual occurrences. What was more, having survived so many perils in the course of their long journey from Belgium to the Willamette, they had come to realize fully that "Divine Providence" was keeping watch over them.

Yet Loyola, speaking on behalf of her five Sisters, could not help remarking that in the two years since leaving Belgium no letter had come to them from Europe; "not a line from either our beloved Sisters or parents." It took, she said, "a strong grace" to bear such a privation so many thousands of miles from all dear and familiar scenes and faces. They had even begun to fear that perhaps the many faithful letters, and the journal she and Sister Aloysia had been keeping for twenty-two months, had somehow gone astray.

"Not so long ago," she reported, "someone carrying mail overland [to St. Louis from the western wilderness] opened mail addressed to the President of the United States!"

It was still "pre-pioneer" days in Oregon when Loyola and the five other Sisters journeyed from Belgium to the Pacific Northwest in the hope of converting to Christianity "the children of the forest," as they called the Red Indians. Through the detailed letters that Loyola and Aloysia so faithfully wrote home to their Mother Superior we can piece together still another story of the almost incredible courage and spirit shown by gently reared women in the early days of the American West.

The names of the six intrepid Sisters from Namur ring a pleasant little tune in the head: Aloysia, Loyola, Albine, Catherine, Cornelia and Norbertine. (Each of them also used, in accordance with the rules of their Order, the name Mary in honor of the Virgin.)

When they started out on their amazing journey there were seven of them, but Sister Mary Reine turned back near the outset of the great adventure. While still in Belgium, waiting for their ship to set sail, Sister Reine chanced to overhear the language of an angry and probably drunken sailor. Unhappily, she understood well the Flemish dialect in which the sailor was shouting. Were men as violent as this to be their crew for many months at sea? Sister Reine promptly "fell into a melancholy and lost heart in her glorious adventure." The Reverend Mother had to come to Ostend to pick her up and take her back to the serene unbroken quiet of the home convent.

The other six adventurers, however, set sail from

Antwerp with resolute hearts. Gay Sister Aloysia managed even to write with humor about the horrors of seasickness which came on them immediately.

"We left the table one after another as if we had been stricken by a sudden blow, and felt our way like little children learning to walk, clinging to chairs, or as best we could to the shoulders of those who were less sick than we. It took us some time to reach the door and then to climb the stairs, where we went on deck to pay our respects to Neptune."

It was the first of many hours of physical discomfort—even agony. Ahead of them stretched seven months of voyage by water—all the way around Cape Horn, twice across the equator. For seven months in high seas and treacherous calm, in freezing cold and suffocating heat, the Sisters were to move about the small deck space allotted to them, hampered by the heavy, full-skirted and bulky garments of their Order.

During the dreary and dangerous weeks of this perilous journey to the other side of the world, their food and water gave out. Rats ate their luggage. Terrifying storms descended on them. Pirates followed them. Sharks and whales threatened the small vessel. For days on end there was no wind to fill the sails of the *Infatigable*. The ship would lie becalmed while captain, crew and passengers waited and prayed for a quickening breeze. When at last the winds came they were sometimes of hurricane velocity. Yet the six gentle nuns survived it all—

even a "miraculous" crossing by the wrong channel of the dread Columbia River bar at their long journey's end.

The first lap of their sea voyage was from Antwerp in Belgium via Calais in France, to Plymouth on the English coast. It was in the English Channel, famous for its turbulent water, that the nuns had their first prostrating experience with seasickness. The pitching vessel allowed no rest by day, or sleep all night long. The ship, wrote Aloysia, "resembled a hospital, the oppressive silence being broken only by the groans of the passengers." Yet the nuns, true to their strict training in unselfish behavior, managed to stagger up from their bunks. Though green and tremulous, exhausted from hours of nausea, they tried to do whatever they could to "relieve" their fellow travelers.

Hardly had they reached the open ocean before the matter of food for the rest of the trip had become of grave concern. An unusual stretch of warm and windless weather—though it was January when they set off—had been enjoyable for the seasick passengers but disastrous for the food supplies. The odor of decaying animal flesh began to permeate the entire vessel. It was finally necessary to throw overboard most of the stores of meat laid in for the seven months at sea. Even the live fowl in the hold had all died, and there would be no possible chance of any fresh purchases before reaching the Pacific coast of South America, many months away!

Thanks, however, to the famed missionary priest, Father de Smet, who was guiding the nuns to the wilderness of the New World, they did have a small supply of fresh milk. In Holland the Father had thoughtfully purchased a goat for the Sisters so that they might enjoy *café au lait* on their journey.

Not one of the Sisters had ever milked before but they set out to learn with the same valiant spirit with which they approached any new experience. One would hold the goat's horns, another would steady the bucket, a third would attempt to draw the milk. Once on a rough day a great wave almost swept a timid milker overboard. She was dashed right to the railing and only saved in the nick of time by a passing sailor. But the milk from that precious if annoying goat came to mean a lot to them all in the days of semi-starvation on shipboard.

Through the entire voyage they had no bread. Even the hard biscuits which were the main staple of their daily diet came to the table with the marks of rats' teeth on them. The hundreds of rats finally grew so bold that they would run right across the dining table while the Sisters were at their meals.

In spite of the constant perils and unending discomfort of the arduous sea voyage to Oregon, the six endearing Sisters knew how to make the most of simple pleasures whenever they came along.

Those two faithful letter writers, Aloysia and Loyola, were keen observers of the sky, the sea, the weather in general. Through their sharp eyes we follow the course of an immense flaming meteor that dropped into the ocean near them, filling them with "speechless awe." We see all six of the young nuns studying the stars, naming the familiar

ones, watching for the strange constellations that appeared over the equator. We share with them their delighted views of the aurora borealis and the dazzling sight of icebergs, mountain high, floating past—a frozen, silent menace, for no one could judge how far beneath the waves their hidden bases might lie.

On calm nights the Sisters often remained on deck to sing their evening hymns. They wrote home to the Reverend Mother about the joy they felt when their soft voices floated in worship over the lightly rolling waves under the first pale stars. "We were still on deck at nine o'clock singing hymns and the Litany of the Blessed Virgin. When we had finished singing, we took delight in contemplating the beauty of the stars. That night the calmness of the sea gave rise to a sense of peace that captivated our hearts and carried us back to the dear home where you are with our Blessed Sisters."

Once as they were singing their twilight hymns a rising breeze suddenly brought within hailing distance a large vessel flying the Dutch flag. The brisk military songs of the soldiers aboard this vessel "contrasted strangely," wrote Loyola, with the nuns' gentle litanies.

Across the waters the Sisters called to ask "from whence they came and wither bound?" "From Rotterdam to Patagonia," came the reply. It was a Dutch prison ship! A shadow fell on the gentle Sisters as the heavily armed vessel with its soldier crew and unfortunate doomed passengers—hidden from sight in the hold—sailed from view in the gathering darkness.

There was another night when they became aware that they were being followed by a most suspicious-looking vessel. The captain himself feared that it was manned by pirates. Pirates would show no mercy, not even to members of the clergy. Of that they were all sure. Even brave Father de Smet could not conceal his alarm. He exhorted the Sisters to pray for their deliverance. A favorable wind sprung up. By a seeming miracle they made their escape.

Of all the perils of the sea in the days of sailing vessels a hurricane was the worst. Off the dangerous coast of Patagonia, bristling with rocks as huge, fierce and pointed as some primeval giants' teeth, they were struck by the most terrible hurricane the crew of the *Infatigable* had ever experienced. For more than a week the wind blew at a rate of seventy to eighty miles an hour. Towering waves came crashing down on the helplessly wallowing vessel.

When by the seventh day, they had lost two sails and part of a mast, Father de Smet and the other priests traveling to Oregon with him gave up hope. They decided to remain on deck all night to await the end.

The Sisters, however, went calmly to bed.

Aloysia, writing in detail to the home convent about the frightening experience of the hurricane winds, reported the intrepidity of Sister Mary Cornelia, reputedly "the most timid of our band." As soon as Father de Smet had left them, after warn-

ing that their end might be near, Cornelia remarked bravely, "I do believe the Reverend Fathers
are easily alarmed. Really the rolling of the vessel
is not any worse than it has heretofore been."

Loyola also wrote about Sister Aloysia and the
hurricane. Aloysia admitted quite honestly that she,
for one, was "seized with terror. But the calm of
resignation to the holy will of God soon succeeded.
I offered up my life and then went peacefully to
bed. 'Ah, dearest Lord,' said I, 'if I die tonight I
shall have to appear before you in night-gown and
cap.'"

As she penned this humorous quotation from
Aloysia one imagines careful Loyola suddenly hesi-
tating. Was this not a bit too flippant for the
Mother Superior to read aloud to her charges?
Surely some modifying phrase was called for! One
can see Loyola biting the end of her quill a moment or two before adding, "A strange reflection
indeed this was, but it did prove that our dear
Sister looked on death without fear."

The storm at last abated. Later they were to
learn that two vessels had gone down at the very
place near Patagonia where they so narrowly
missed shipwreck themselves.

Eager Sister Aloysia had as much pleasure in
studying the ways of tropical fish seen from the
ship's narrow deck as Mary Walker had from
studying the rocks and plants on her horseback
journey to the far West.

Aloysia found European fish and tropical fish
very different altogether. "In Europe the fish are

quiet, peaceable, graceful. This can be said of the salmon, trout, codfish, carp and other creatures of the finny tribe. But in the tropics, each time that the denizens of the deep make their appearance, we are convulsed with laughter, so ludicrous do

they appear to us. Some seem to be all tail, others all head, and some have the head where one would expect the tail to be."

But surely the most fun the six brave nuns had on the entire journey came when they crossed the equator. Crossing the equatorial line has always been an occasion for traditional sport on the part of ships' crews from the distant past to today. The presence of priests and nuns aboard did not deter the sailors of the *Infatigable* from enjoying the few hours of rough amusement allowed them in their hard lives.

For the pleasure of the cloistered Sisters left behind in Namur, Aloysia described in full detail the high-jinks of the crew.

It was seven in the evening, she wrote, when from their quarters they heard the sailors crying out in loud cheerful voices: "The Fire of Neptune! The Fire of Neptune!"

The excited Sisters hurried up to the deck to see what was happening.

About a hundred feet from the ship they saw an immense column of fire. The sailors had lighted a cask of dried peas and tar and thrown it into the ocean where it was burning brightly.

As the Sisters stood gazing at "Neptune's Fire," a solemn voice was heard to cry loudly from the topmast:

"Captain, have you any passengers aboard?"

The captain, a brave and cheerful man whom the Sisters had learned to their sorrow was in the last stages of tuberculosis, cried out in a merry voice, "I have twelve."

"Do they intend to pass the line?"

"Aye."

"Well, tomorrow Neptune in person will administer baptism which must be experienced by all who pass the line."

When they crossed the equator at ten that night a flame was burned from the topmast. At ten the next morning another cry sounded throughout the ship: "Neptune! Neptune!"

This time the Sisters remained discreetly below, though they managed to get a view of Neptune in a great wig and coarse flax beard, carrying a huge wooden compass and sextant. The God of the Sea performed a comic pantomime of the captain taking longitude. With Neptune was a member of the crew disguised as "Neptune's wife." Attending them both was a guard of honor bearing wooden swords, tridents and spears. These sailors had smeared their faces with tar, and presented to the peeping nuns "a most hideous aspect."

Although no one molested the hidden Sisters, the Reverend Fathers did not entirely escape. They had been formally invited to join the captain on the bridge for the ceremony. Neptune, backed by his guard, demanded that all the priests, including Father de Smet, allow themselves to be shaved. There was nothing to do but submit. After this ceremony, the final "baptism" was administered: a sudden deluge of water from somewhere high above that thoroughly wetted everyone in sight.

During all the long slow weeks at sea the ravenous rats had grown so desperate that they finally gnawed away the side support beams of the vessel to the "thickness of a sheet of paper." When the *Infatigable* came in sight of the South American port of Valparaiso, the captain decided to make a stopover for repairs and at the same time attempt to rid his vessel of these unwelcome rodent traveling companions, now numbering no less than 1400!

The stopover in Valparaiso gave the Sisters a welcome chance to set foot again on land, the first time in ninety-two days. They had not realized what the sight of lamps shining from the windows of houses would mean to them until they saw the lights of Valparaiso across the twilit bay. They were moved to tears.

When they went ashore in the morning they found, to their surprise, a group of French nuns waiting to greet them. These French Sisters "vied with one another" to extend hospitality to the little Belgian group bound on an even more hazardous venture and one much further from home.

After Valparaiso, the Sisters enjoyed one more respite from ship life. This was in the Peruvian capital of Lima.

Lima was to be the last stop before the dreaded climax of the journey—the crossing of the perilous Columbia River bar. In Lima the captain hoped to get some accurate information about how best to make this crossing, still far away, up the rocky Pacific coast.

The Sisters, hoping to prepare themselves for this last and most fearful of their many trials, had planned to spend their time in Lima in silence and prayer. Nothing came of these careful plans, however, for the attentive ladies of this rich and beautiful city would not let them alone. A certain Señora Rivodera insisted that they accept an "urgent invitation to visit her *hacienda*" in the country outside the capital. Other attentive ladies came bringing gifts of fruit: "dates, *pillas, chilimoya* and *pignas.*"

The nuns were to think longingly of this fruit in the weeks to come when again contrary winds kept them at sea until the last ham of their new supplies had to be eaten although "in such a state of decomposition that the odor was insupportable" and their supply of water was almost gone.

The Sisters decided then that prayers must surely have ceased for them back home in Belgium. They had been gone so long, they agreed, that everyone thought them safely at their destination. "Our Sisters believe that we are already in Oregon, while we are still battling with an angry sea."

It was the 29th of July, 1844, when they came at last to the long-awaited climax of their arduous trip. They were face to face with the necessity of crossing the bar of the Columbia River, "that dreaded bar, the terror of all travelers to Oregon" approaching from the sea side.

In writing about this perilous passage of the Columbia bar, Aloysia no doubt pictured the Reverend Mother and the other Sisters in Namur listening by candlelight in the peaceful quiet of the old convent to a description of a thrilling adventure utterly unlike any they would ever have or could even imagine.

"A dense fog hung over the mouth of the river

whose waters were dashing in uncontrolled fury
into the surging sea. Enormous breakers lashed
themselves into foam the whole length of the bar,
and as we gazed upon them from our storm-beaten
vessel with its tattered sails and broken masts, the
thought uppermost in our minds was, 'Will she be
able to make her way?' "

It seemed unlikely. The Sisters, worn now with
long travel, constant danger and improper food,
had to fight despair. Yet when, by that first evening, it was clear no passage would be possible before dark, if at all, Sister Loyola, representing her
five companions, went to Father de Smet to assure
him that the nuns would gladly—if this seemed the
will of Providence—return to Lima where they had
discovered that trained Sisters were also badly
needed.

This was far from an easy offering for the six
nuns to make. In undertaking the perilous Oregon
mission in the first place, they had made a great
individual sacrifice, a personal offering to God. It
would have deeply disturbed and disappointed them
not to be allowed to complete the sacrifice as they
had so long hoped and planned.

Through the night the nuns remained in almost
constant prayer. The next day was the 31st of
July, the feast day of St. Ignatius Loyola, to whom
they now made special offering. And then they
"saw a sign." Far off they caught a glimpse of a
two-masted vessel. They had expected to see the
three masts of a warship guarding the entrance to
Oregon, which was still at that time disputed territory between England and America. These two

masts seemed to the Sisters an omen of good fortune. To their pious minds, those two bars suggested the iconography of St. Loyola. They became
convinced that their prayers to this saint would be
answered. They would cross over in safety.

But before they could reach the quiet waters lying beyond the raging bar many tense and anxious
hours were to pass. The ship's mate had, since
early morning of the 31st, been begging the captain to make a run for it. The captain, though a
dying man himself, did not choose to imperil the
lives of his passengers and he steadfastly refused to
listen to the mate's entreaties.

At last, however, when the mate would not give
up, the captain consented to allow him to go out
in a small boat and make a survey of the situation.

A boat was lowered over the side. At once it
disappeared in the churning waves. Everyone gave
up the mate for lost. But sometime later he reap-
peared alongside. The boat was hoisted to the deck
and the mate assured the captain that the ship
could safely proceed, for there were at least thirty
feet of water under them.

The mate was lying but the captain did not
know it. He ordered the sails of the *Infatigable*
spread at once. Slowly the sea-beaten vessel began
to advance towards the mouth of the Columbia.

The sky was cloudless. It was a beautiful day
"with more brilliant sunshine than we had seen for
many days," wrote Aloysia. It did not seem a likely
scene for death, which it nearly proved to be.

The Sisters, after prayers, climbed to the bridge.

They looked again at the ominous line of surf, five miles in length, where the heavy seas were breaking on the sand bar over which they must somehow pass. They also saw a fierce reef of rocks. But their faith in their safety now remained firm.

When the *Infatigable* finally reached the surging breakers of the bar, two sailors were lashed to the sides of the ship in order to give soundings of the water's depths.

"Seven fathoms," came the first cry.

A thrill of icy terror shot through everyone at this news. Seven fathoms was far too shallow for passage! The ship must surely founder!

Scarcely a moment passed before the second cry came. "Six fathoms!"

Then, hardly before they had time to gasp, "Five!"

And almost instantly, "Three!"

The captain, giving way at this point to his pent-up emotion, cried out wildly, "We are between life and death!"

But then, "Four fathoms!" cried the two men lashed to the ship's sides in the whirling spray.

Hope revived again, but only for an instant.

"Three fathoms!" came the cry for the second time. The ship had reached the impassable shallows and they were still easily two miles from the safe waters that were their destination. Here they would surely founder and break to pieces in the surf and on the hidden rocks.

At this point, the mate who had told the lie about the channel's depth cried out to the captain, loud enough for all to hear, "We have made a

mistake, sir. The river divides into two branches and we have taken the wrong one."

At this seemingly hopeless news the stout captain rallied all his forces. He called out in sudden defiance, "Bah! The *Infatigable* passes everywhere. Advance!"

They advanced, awaiting death. The Sisters prayed with the Reverend Fathers. In five minutes they found themselves, without knowing quite how, at rest in the calm river.

Around four o'clock that afternoon as the Sisters were having some much needed coffee they saw their first Indian canoe approaching the vessel. The Indians came aboard in a state of respectful awe. Their chief told the captain, speaking through an interpreter, that no vessel had ever entered the river by the route the *Infatigable* had taken. It was known, from experience, to be "impassable." As the Indians had watched the ship from the far bank, they had believed it would surely be dashed to pieces and all its passengers lost. As was customary in the presence of death they had stood there, wrote Loyola, "rending their garments" as a sign of grief.

The ship's plight had also been witnessed the night before by the Governor of Astoria. Taking some Indian helpers, he had hastened to Cape Disappointment to light a beacon which he had hoped would attract the crew's attention and help guide them. The crew had seen the light but feared it might be a snare set by hostile Indians to lure them to destruction. When daylight came the Governor, seeing the ship still in the wrong channel, had hoisted a white flag and fired guns. But no one on shipboard could hear the guns owing to the noise of the water, and the white flag was not visible to them in the spray-drenched sunshine.

More Indians came aboard that first day. Clatsops and Chinooks, traditional enemies, tried hard to behave themselves properly in the presence of these miracle-working strangers. The nuns gave all the Indian visitors hot coffee to drink—they had nothing else to offer. Towards evening the chief of the Clatsops sent a gift of fresh salmon and new potatoes—a most welcome relief to everyone after so many weeks of salt meat and hard tack.

Then, at last, the Sisters were taken ashore. And here they gave way to the joy of finding themselves on land again, a land they now considered "home" for they never expected to leave this primitive wilderness or the "children of the forest" they had come to teach. Yet there were no homesick thoughts about Namur, no backward glances to their Belgian homeland, only joy and gratitude at feeling solid ground beneath their feet once more.

Very few white people were scattered through the vastness of the Oregon country in those years.

Those who were near enough hastened to entertain the brave Sisters from far-away Europe. They were invited to dine first with Captain Birnie, the dignified Governor of Astoria who had tried his best to warn them of the ship's danger. Captain Birnie had a spirited, capable half-breed wife and seven beautiful daughters. At the Birnies' at dinner, the Sisters ate their first native berry pie. *Délicieuse,"* they wrote to the Reverend Mother back in Namur.

After Astoria they journeyed on up-river to Fort Vancouver and there, like Narcissa Whitman nine years before, they enjoyed the lavish hospitality of that genial "international host," John McLoughlin, who was still dwelling in feudal splendor at this stronghold of the British Hudson's Bay Company.

From Fort Vancouver the six nuns departed in small boats up the Willamette River to the site of their future mission.

The first night out of Vancouver the nuns camped on the shore and ate their supper camp-style around a glowing fire, just as people have always done along the waterways and trails of the American West.

By now thoroughly relaxed from the tensions of their long voyage, they carried on among themselves as gayly as schoolgirls. Aloysia was undoubtedly glad to give the Reverend Mother a picture of them at ease at last, out of danger, and able to laugh and "let go."

"Although we had but the ground for table and our heels for chairs, our appetites were not in the least impaired. Supper being finished Bishop Blanchet said the evening prayer aloud, to which the whole camp responded. We then sang the Litany of the Blessed Virgin and withdrew to our improvised canvas convent. As it was not yet nine o'clock we profited of the interim to laugh to our hearts' content."

And who of the six was the drollest, and who laughed the loudest? Although it is Aloysia writing, one feels certain it was she who had them all in stitches.

It is tantalizing when one reads the faithful letters and journals of these remarkable Sisters to try to picture them to oneself. Very little that is directly descriptive or pictorial of the six nuns can be found in these chronicles of the simple and hazardous events through which they passed so valiantly.

Of Mary Cornelia we do know that it was she who, though reputedly "the most timid," had shown herself so staunch at the time of the week's hurricane off Patagonia. In one of the letters home we also learn that Cornelia invariably "led by love, triumphed by tenderness." Plainly she was a gentle and lovable soul. She was also a very hard worker. When the Sisters arrived at the deserted, half-ruined buildings at St. Paul, once a mission of priests on the banks of the lonely Willamette, Cornelia is described "trying to find the floor of the church under the crust of dirt that covers it."

Of dignified Loyola, the five nuns' Superior, who wrote such informative letters home, we know that she was a tower of superhuman strength in all emergencies. It was said of her that she was "more than a woman" and could "toil terribly." This, however, would hardly have set her apart among the six of them, all of whom worked, as Mary Richardson and Narcissa Whitman were doing at the very same time, every waking hour and far into the night because there was so much to do and so few hands to do it.

Sister Mary Catherine referred to herself as a *"bouche-trou,"* a French term for jack-of-all-trades. Her greatest accomplishment was an ability to "do sums," which is to say, arithmetic. Mary Catherine could add, subtract and divide with ease for she had had in her youth the rare opportunity, in a home of wealth and education, to share a tutor with her brothers. But her aristocratic background naturally had no effect on her drudgery at the Oregon mission. There was more to do here than arithmetic! It was she who took charge of all the laundry and could regularly be seen, so the letters tell us, "alone for the washing in the shade of a venerable oak."

As for Sister Mary Albine, she "possessed a taste for needlework." Her deft fingers, accustomed to the finest Belgian embroidery, were henceforth to be employed in teaching ignorant Indian women how to make the simplest, coarsest and most modest of garments.

Sister Norbertine had won the Oregon trip in part because of her skill as a gardener. (You must remember that many other Sisters had volunteered for the great honor of this dangerous mission. All had to have special qualifications besides an eagerness to make the sacrifice.) Norbertine's "capacity for agriculture, evinced in the garden at Ghent,"

was to stand them all in good stead when they began to plant their precious seeds in the rich, untouched soil near the mission. It was Norbertine
who helped produce the melons and the cucumbers
from which the snakes, wolves and wild horses had
to be kept!

Thanks to Norbertine's expert green thumb the
nuns were soon harvesting potatoes and pumpkins,
turnips and peas, leafy green vegetables, even
meadow barley for the cows they had acquired.
They set out fruit trees and planted chicory to sup-
plement their coffee supply. The country itself was
rich in native fruits. A larder of berries, edible
roots, and varieties of nuts lay ready to hand, and
indeed the Sisters jokingly referred to the adjoining
forests and meadows as their "pantry."

So there they were on the Willamette in wild
Oregon—Aloysia, Loyola, Albine, Catherine, Cornelia and Norbertine. All of them were carpentering, painting, gardening, mending, sewing, milking,
forming bucket brigades from the river to water
their vegetables in dry spells, teaching the sign of
the Cross and simple prayers to their little red-
skinned charges. They were also teaching them—
and their mothers as well—to wash their faces daily
and keep the vermin out of their hair. In time,
they began instruction in knitting and sewing and
cooking the "white" way, and even eventually
taught some of them to read a little. And all the
while the nuns were studying, in their own "spare
moments," not only Chinook but English!

The neighboring Indians were friendly but lazy.

The children had to be lured into performing simple tasks by special devices. There was no quick automatic obedience to a nun's wish or command, as there would have been among children back home in Belgium.

Loyola wrote about a successful ruse of hers for getting wood carried.

"We are now," said she to her little Indian pupils whom she was also instructing in religious rites, "going on a pilgrimage and will start out by singing a canticle. When we reach the end of the enclosure, we shall each take an armful of wood and carry it to the house."

The Indian children, who always loved an occasion for singing, were eager to play this new game. The first pilgrimage from woodpile to shed was in honor of God the Father, the second was in honor of God the Son, the third in honor of God the Holy Ghost. "The pilgrimage had so much attraction for them that when the bell rang for lunch they were not satisfied until I promised them that we would afterwards make others in honor of the Blessed Virgin and St. Joseph." So Loyola got in the wood supply!

Since the Indians entered with zest into all forms of ceremonies, the wise nuns celebrated as best they could every Catholic feast day, holiday and festival they had known in Europe. Before long not only the Indian children but their fathers and mothers were also eagerly begging to play roles on these occasions. At the celebration of Sister Loyola's "name day" the "central feature" was a piece of religious theatre having to do with "the Creation of the World, the Fall of Our First Parents, and the Redemption." (Reading of this scene in an entry of the nuns' journals, one could wish for a movie camera and a tape recorder!)

Within a matter of weeks after their arrival the Sisters had wrought such a transformation in the old, half-demolished church that Bishop Blanchet, coming on a visit, could scarce credit his senses. The Sisters had found the roughly-built mission sagging, broken and dirty. But even its sad condition held meaning for the six nuns. "Not a bad resemblance to the stable at Bethlehem," they remarked, reminding themselves bravely of the lowly birthplace of Jesus. Before long, after many scrubbings, they could tack bright colored pictures to the plain wooden walls. They decorated wherever possible with "loot" from the forest; "graceful festoons, trailing vines, wild blossoms." They made a little chapel to the Virgin Mary and hung it with plain white muslin, through which "the wind entered in unrestrained freedom." They put precious colored paper from Belgium on the front of the altar and draped the tabernacle with two old curtains from one of the Namur classrooms.

When all was done they stood and regarded their handiwork with pleasure. They had created beauty with the very simplest means. "The altar of our Lady at Namur is not so beautiful as this," declared Aloysia, sighing with satisfaction. Into all their minds, at Aloysia's remark, there must have rushed memories of the famed beauties of the old medieval churches they had known in their years in Belgium. But they all hastened to agree with enthusiastic Aloysia.

"Nor at Ghent, either," Sister Norbertine loyally added.

Even matter-of-fact Loyola was moved to say, "Nor at Ixelles." ·

Loyola has left a description of the nuns and their little charges on a day in high summer. They had gone on a picnic, leaving Sister Catherine and Sister Albine at home to "keep house." And now we see the little Indians giving gratifying proof to the Sisters of the improvement in their manners. They help the Sisters up the hills. They draw aside the low-hanging branches of the trees that make walking difficult. They run here and there, away from their patient teachers and back again with eager questions and sometimes even with "offering of their reflections which are rather wise for little Indian girls," said Loyola. They fill cups with the sweet and fragrant wild strawberries hiding in the grass of open meadows. They strip fruit from the many kinds of berry bushes growing wild in Oregon. They gather nosegays to present to the nuns, or to take home for the image of their favorite saint: flat-petaled wild rose, spears of blue iris, wild currant, violets, lilies.

At noon the four Sisters found a large pine tree with a lovely carpet of needles at its base. Here they sat down to spread their lunch, and here, just as they were opening their hamper, who should arrive but "old Baptiste," the halfbreed French Canadian man-of-all-work whom they now had at their

mission. And what had Baptiste brought but hot pancakes sent on for the picnic by Sister Catherine and Sister Albine!

And here we shall leave the intrepid nuns from Namur, resting under a pine *"gigantesque"* with their little Indian pupils who, putting aside their wilted nosegays, washing their berry-stained hands in a nearby stream, are sitting down to enjoy, for the first time in their lives, the novel taste of French pancakes on an Oregon picnic.

CHAPTER SIX

THE PROPHET

*I*T was fifteen years after Narcissa Whitman rode with her husband across the plains and mountains of the unexplored American continent that a young girl of seventeen, named Abigail Scott, set out with her family from a village in Illinois bound on the long western journey.

The Scotts' house in Illinois stood within a few hundred feet of a main highway, then little more than a rough dirt road, that passed between the towns of Pekin and Peoria. Along this road there had begun to pass during every spring and summer of the late 1840s long lines of covered wagons moving westward.

Abigail could remember all her life the children of these emigrants, barefooted and often dirty, who would come at sundown to the Scott house bringing sticks of hickory or walnut in order to carry off to their own campfires some of the live coals that her mother kept covered with ashes on the

hearth all day long to make her own cooking easier. Mrs. Scott always gave generously of her fire
for the sake of the poor homeless women—whom
she very much pitied—camping out down the road,
with a brood of children and a restless husband.

Not all the people who passed the Scott property
were bound for the Pacific Ocean. Many, coming
out of Kentucky, Indiana, Iowa, and other parts of
Illinois, planned to go no farther than Missouri,
then considered part of the "Far West." But Abigail's father's imagination was fired, like that of
many other men of the time, by the thought of
the distant land of the Pacific Northwest. He
caught "Oregon fever" in a bad way.

Abigail's mother did not wish to leave her home
in Illinois. Physically frail, worn out with the bearing of a large family of children and too much
heavy work, she both dreaded and feared the long
uncertain journey. Her protests were, however, in
vain. It was Mr. Scott who made the decisions for
the family and his mind was made up. In 1851,
over the mother's desperate pleas to remain where
they were, the family packed everything they were
able to carry, and set off on the long uncertain
journey.

Her mother's unwillingness to go west, and the
seemingly little influence this had on her father,
were to affect Abigail deeply. It may even be fair
to surmise that they were partly responsible for the
fact that some years later Abigail became a "Suffragette," and went forth to preach the doctrine of
"Equal Rights for Women."

All Mrs. Scott's fears and apprehensions were

realized on the exhausting and difficult westward
trek. Tired and frail, she succumbed easily to the
cholera epidemic that was raging then along the
trail of the emigrants. Her untimely death was a
blow from which none of her children ever quite
recovered.

Abigail brooded long on the fact that her mother's
wishes had seemed to count for so little. As she
brooded she remembered the day when she had
gone into her mother's room to greet a newborn
sister. She had found her mother weeping. "Poor
baby," she had said, "she'll be a woman some day.
Poor baby. A woman's lot is so hard."

Why was a woman's lot so hard? Abigail was to
ask herself this question many times in the years
to come and when she finally had the answer she
decided to do something about it.

Abigail, who was to make words her tools
throughout a long and useful life, began to show
her talents at an early age. When, an old lady in
a lace cap, she wrote the story of her dramatic
and busy life, she recalled how as a mere child she
had been so fired by the "log cabin and hard
cider" campaign of William Henry Harrison that
she had stood on a stump in her Illinois village to
harangue her playmates about "Tippecanoe and
Tyler too."

Like Mary Walker, Abigail was an avid reader.
Although she had been told that nothing could be
taken to Oregon in a wagon train worth less than
a "dollar a pound" (a high figure for those days)
she managed to smuggle into the Scotts' covered

wagon a copy of Webster's *Elementary Speller*. On the way west she was already making use of this book, as Mary Walker used her geology and botany. For Abigail was keeping a journal of the plains trip. She tried to write in it every day no matter how tired, sad, or anxious she was.

After they got to Oregon, Abigail was able at once to get a job teaching school. But very soon she was married to a neighboring farmer named Ben Duniway. On her marriage she had to give up teaching to become, as she bitterly said, "a servant without wages."

Abigail, though not frail in mind, spirit or will-power, was—like her mother—frail in body. And like her mother she found herself caught in an endless round of work that was too heavy for her; scrubbing, milking, churning, sewing, canning—not only for her children, her husband, and the hired men, but also for assorted bachelor friends of Ben's who liked to drop in at mealtimes at what Abigail sometimes called in despair "the Duniway hotel."

By a curious turn of fate Abigail's opportunity to show what she really had in her came as a result of seeming ill fortune.

One day while she was plucking a goose for feathers for pillows and beds (for there was no ready-made bedding in those days) a man came to call on her husband. Abigail overheard their conversation. The man was asking Ben to sign his name to a note which would allow the man to borrow a large sum of money.

When she heard her husband agreeing to this

proposal, Abigail went into the room to protest.
She knew that, if the man was not able to pay up
when the note fell due, Ben would lose his farm
which he was putting up as security. But her husband would not listen to her. Women were not
supposed to understand business details. This was a
man's world. Ben went right ahead and signed the
note.

In time Abigail's worst fears came to pass. The
note fell due. The man could not pay. Ben Duniway had to put up the money and, in order to
raise it, he had to sell the farm and everything
they owned.

When the sheriff came to serve the papers that
let the Duniways know they were to be sued if
they didn't pay the man's note, Ben was not at
home. Abigail, who had had no legal right to pre-
vent the signing of the note (since a woman at
that time had no legal position of any kind) found,
however, that the sheriff, in her husband's absence,
could make her accept and sign the papers he had
come to serve. This seemed to her the highest form
of injustice.

It was all a part of a process, however, that she
referred to later as "opening her eyes."

When Ben sold the farm, the Duniway family,
now penniless, moved to the little town of Lafay-
ette. And here the second serious blow struck them.
Ben was injured in an accident with a runaway
horse. He could never do farm work again and
farming was all he knew. It now fell to Abigail's
lot to earn the income for the whole family.

She returned, not without a certain joy, to teaching school. Although she had to rise at three in summer and four in winter to clean house and prepare breakfast for her six children, her husband and the boarders she had taken in to help make ends meet, she did not complain. She was interested in her work. She found that she could even "rest" a little when she taught the primary classes. But not with the upper divisions. (She taught everyone from six to sixteen!) She had little chance to study at home and had to count on her own native intelligence to work out, as they came along, the problems she presented to her older pupils.

Abigail was a hard-headed realist. Although education was more important to her than anything else in the world, she soon found she could not make a living at it. She saw that if she was to continue as the family's main support she must somehow get into business.

She decided to move her family to the nearby larger town of Albany. Here she turned her schoolhouse into a store with counters, shelves and showcases. She had managed to save thirty dollars and with this sum to spend on "goods" she journeyed to Portland to interview the town's richest merchant, Jacob Meier.

Mr. Meier, a man both kind and astute, insisted that she take $1,200 worth of goods on credit. Abigail's head whirled. She had come to Portland with thirty dollars and was being offered more than a thousand! Should she plunge? Did she dare to? She decided to plunge.

In just three weeks she was back, her entire debt paid. This time she asked for $3,000 worth of goods and got it without a question.

It was millinery, oddly enough, that led Abigail out farther and farther into life. In her prosperous shop, to which women began to come from all the neighboring villages and farms of the countryside, she had a chance to meet and talk to women from every kind of life and many different backgrounds. What she saw of the women around her led Abigail to remark with wry humor, "Half of us are dolls, half of us are drudges, and all of us are fools."

The thing that upset her the most was the part she was asked to play in little games of deceit by which women—who had in those days no allowance of any kind and no financial independence—deceived their husbands about money. A woman would, for instance, pretend to her husband that she was buying cheap straw hats for her children at Abigail's shop and, when his back was turned, persuade Abigail to exchange the hats for more practical and also more expensive ones. The woman would go into debt for her children's hats and then pay off the debt bit by bit by pilfering small change from her husband's pockets when he was asleep.

When Abigail, horrified and troubled by this kind of experience, went to another merchant of the town to talk to him about such a shocking state of affairs, he only laughed at her and said, "We merchants couldn't make any profit on fancy

goods at all if it wasn't for what the women steal from their husbands."

This did not seem a very satisfactory answer to Abigail. She went on thinking her troubled thoughts about the wrongness of the whole situation. It was true that women stole from their husbands, but the men stole from their wives too. Only in the case of the men there was a difference. When, for instance, a man helped himself to his wife's precious "butter money" or "egg money"—the one kind of small savings that country women had a right to in those days by a sort of unspoken law, since it was the women who did the churning and raised the hens —*he* did not need to do it in the dark of the night. He just helped himself and he had a "legal" right to do so, for everything his wife owned "legally" belonged to him.

In the book called *Path Breaking* that Abigail wrote about her life and how she came to be a Suffragette, she tells a story of a local farmer who took his wife's long-hoarded butter money to buy himself a race horse, a luxury that he did not need. The poor woman had promised her children new waterproof outfits to wear to school in the rainy Oregon winters. She had planned to use her butter money for the purchase. When this money had been taken without her consent, she came to Abigail in tears asking for a job of "plain sewing." She wanted to keep her promise to her children. The woman was ill and already overworked. Abigail had no job for her. In a year the woman was dead. When Abigail heard how people were offering "condolences" to the "bereaved" husband, who was still riding his fine new race horse, Abigail's blood fairly boiled.

Plainly something was terribly wrong! But what to do about it—that was the question.

It was not long before Abigail had become the confidante of the whole countryside. Women who were in trouble of any kind took to coming straight to her to talk it out. She remembered all her life another unhappy woman whose husband was a drunkard. Whatever the man earned he promptly spent in the nearest saloon. Finally he deserted his wife and family and left town. Abigail helped this woman set herself up in a boarding house to support her now fatherless children. (To run a boarding house was quite respectable in the early West where the matter of housing for all the newcomers pouring into a pioneer land was a vital problem.) After Abigail had helped the woman start a new life for herself and her family, the drunken husband returned. Still within his "legal" rights he took all the money she had saved, mortgaged the family furniture again, and once again left town.

Abigail did a lot of thinking and talking, and even a good deal of fuming, over things of this kind and the general lot of women. She was thirty-six years old when, as she said, finally "the light broke" on her. She always gave her husband, Ben, the full credit for pointing out the truth to her. One day as she was protesting some injustice he put his hand fondly on the top of her head and told her she could go on fuming all she pleased about the "slavery of women" but nothing could change until all women had "the right to vote and equal rights with men before the law."

It is not easy today, when people like Abigail Duniway and others of her kind have made it possible for all women to vote, to have an education, to earn money in jobs and professions, to have a right to their own money and to their own property and all the rest of the things now taken for granted, to realize just what it meant in Abigail's day to declare oneself in favor of "Equal Rights"; to become that dreaded kind of female, a "Suffragette."

Suffragettes were already making a stir in the Eastern part of the United States. They were considered by most people to be "freaks" or "fiends" and all, without exception, were said to be "man haters." The truth is that most of them came from fine backgrounds, were handsome, gentle-voiced, educated, and dedicated.

But Abigail knew what she was in for if she openly stated that she believed that women should have Equal Rights, including, above all, the right to vote. She had already been sent an anonymous valentine that had made her cry. The valentine showed a trembling "henpecked" husband, crouched down as if in terror: "clambering over him were a lot of squalling children, and above his cowering form stood an irate, illy-clad, toothless, straggle-haired woman, brandishing a broom." Under the picture there appeared these lines:

"Fiend, devil's imp, or what you will
You surely your poor man will kill,
With luckless days and sleepless nights,
Haranguing him with Woman's Rights!"

Ben Duniway laughed Abigail out of her tears and it was not long before she was able to handle such an insult in a new and more effective way. On another Valentine's Day she was seated on a public platform, prepared to make a speech about Women's Rights, when a page came up and handed her, in front of everyone in the audience, a large envelope. Abigail opened it and unfolded a bright-colored poster. It was a picture very like the one she had received in her home some years before.

This time Abigail did not cry. She laughed. She walked to the front of the platform and exhibited the valentine for everyone to see. "The author of this exquisite work of art didn't give his name, but he has sent along his picture," she said. The audience burst out laughing. "You see," she went on, "that it represents a henpecked husband. He is lying on his back, on the floor, a picture of terror. Over him stands his wife, half-hen and half-woman. Her beak is clutching a few straggling hairs on the top of his head. I know the poor artist doesn't intend to represent *my* husband, for *he* isn't bald-headed."

When everyone had had a good laugh Abigail folded up the cruel and ugly poster and said simply, "Don't you see that all we have to do, when we meet the nettle of ridicule, is to grasp it tightly, and then it cannot sting us much?"

When Abigail had committed herself to becoming a fighter in the Cause of Equal Rights she gave up her Albany store and moved with her family to Portland, the largest town in the state. She had a new plan. She was going to found a newspaper. Her brother, Harvey Scott, had become the editor of the *Oregonian*, the leading newspaper of that part of the country. But she did not turn to him for any help or advice. She simply rented two bedrooms in a plain frame house, hired a foreman at twenty-five dollars a week, set her sons to learning printing, and was soon embarked on the next stage of her career. Only when the paper was well launched did she invite Harvey in to have a look. His sincere praise and surprise warmed her heart.

She called her newspaper *The New Northwest*. In the same year that she founded it, the great feminist, Susan B. Anthony, came to the Pacific Coast from New York State to talk on Women's Rights.

Since the end of the Civil War Susan B. Anthony had been talking to women everywhere—and men too—about the fact that Abraham Lincoln had himself said, when he freed the slaves and gave them the right to vote, that "equality" belonged to all Americans, "and by no means excluding women." But even these words of a great President had not yet given women equality nor kept those who preached the new doctrine from being badly treated. Once when Miss Anthony had

dared—back in New York State where she lived—
to go to the polls and try to vote she had been
fined $100 for her crime!

So when the famous (some said "infamous") Miss
Anthony came to the Far West and Abigail Duniway became her manager during her visit, curious
people began to buy *The New Northwest* hoping to
read about the dangerous "doings" of these two
frightening "man haters." The circulation of Abigail's paper boomed.

But Abigail was much too astute to fill her
newspaper simply with propaganda. She always
said that her life as a milliner had taught her a
lot about the psychology of the average woman.
She believed that she could best interest women in
the problem of their legal "rights" by dealing also
with such everyday matters as how long skirts were
going to be that year, how you could cut over an
out-of-date dress, how you could make mutton stew
more appetizing. So she began a Free Advice to
Readers column.

In this column she never hesitated to express her
own personal views. Sometimes, reading fading cop-
ies of *The New Northwest,* one cannot help smiling:
"You need not make a skirt with a train. Hope
you are going to be a sensible helpmate to your
future husband and, if so, you must begin by dress-
ing sensibly. A trailing skirt is an emblem of deg-
radation."

Thus, subtly, Abigail kept hammering away on
the theme of equality and on the theme of women
"growing up" to their full stature.

She entertained her readers also with continued

stories that she wrote herself: *Ellen Dowd, the Farmer's Wife, Judith Reid, the Plain Story of a Plain Woman.* These drew for material on her own experiences as a struggling young housewife and mother. Women liked to read these stories because they found mirrored in their simple plots the kind of experience they too were having.

It was inevitable that Abigail, with her gift of words and her fiery interest in the subject of Women's Rights, should soon take to the public platform. To do such a thing was the most shocking step so far. Not many years before she herself became a public speaker, Abigail had been hissed for daring to enter a hall on her husband's arm just to listen to a male lecturer!

Abigail of course realized that as a woman speaker, traveling alone, "talking in public," she would be considered a greater "freak" than ever. But she was willing to face this new ridicule if by so doing she could plant the seeds of rebellion in other feminine hearts, or make men too "see the light." For Abigail, always a realist, knew very well that it was men who would finally decide the question of votes for women. Men alone had the right to vote and they alone could grant this privilege to their wives, sisters, daughters and mothers— or forever keep it from them. She also always felt that the women of the Far West would be the first to win the vote because they had so clearly shown —in the days of the great emigrations—just what stuff they were made of and how they could equal men in enduring danger and hardships.

Before long Abigail had become a familiar figure

on river boats and stagecoaches of the pioneer period. With her strong handsome face under its con-
servative but always smart and expensive hat (Abigail was aware of the importance of such details!),
with her "sensible" shoes to make walking easier,
her neat gloves, her inevitable umbrella (sometimes
useful as a weapon of defense), she would buy a
ticket on one of the comfortable boats that made
their slow way up the Columbia River from the
green seacoast to the dry inland country. When the
steamer reached the sluggish parts of the river
where there were no rapids to excite the passengers
and where the scenery had become monotonous,
Abigail would ask the captain's permission to make
a speech. She had found that passengers would listen to anyone when they were bored—and besides,
Equal Rights was hardly a boring subject! People
felt strongly on it one way or another! When she
had finished her little talk she would, with quiet
dignity, take up a collection "for the cause." When
the steamer tied up for the night at some riverside
village Abigail would bravely go ashore, alone, a
strange woman, in a strange town, and try to find
a room large enough in which to hold another
meeting, make another speech.

She had great courage and a sense of humor.
Without these traits of her character she could
never have survived. She was able even to see the
irony in the fact that the Pixley Sisters—with a
"daring," even "shocking" song-and-dance act—
could get a hall in any town sooner than she with
her dignfied talks on suffrage for women.

Sometimes enlightened clergymen opened their

churches to her, but even in a church she was not necessarily free of hecklers. Once a choir of women was organized to sing her down. They kept rising and bursting into a hymn every time Abigail got to her feet to speak. When the hymn was over Abigail would rise again. The choir would then also rise and start singing once more. Abigail would sit and patiently wait. After half an hour of this give-and-take, the choir, seeing it was getting nowhere (except growing hoarse!) decided to sing the *Doxology*, the hymn which signalizes the end of services in certain Protestant churches. At this the church was cleared—and Abigail was left without any audience.

She spoke in stores, in schools, in hotel lobbies, in private houses, in blacksmiths' shops, in stables, even once in the back room of a saloon. (That was on a night when the key of the hall she had engaged had mysteriously "disappeared.") By the yellow light of kerosene lamps she would stand in quiet dignity making her vivid pictures—and Abigail, the word-user, knew how to describe injustice in the lives of women. Over and over she would stress the unfairness of the fact that the women who bore the country's children still had no legal right to decide the laws of the land to which these children belonged.

One of the favorite questions often put to timid women who had begun to think they really did have a right to the vote and might like to exercise that right, was the silly question, "But how would you like to serve on a jury and be locked in a room with eleven men?" The very idea was "indecent." "Indecent!" Abigail would cry. "Is it more indecent than the fact that though women may not sit on juries, juries can try them for their very lives?"

Another standard argument of the period was that if women voted they should also be willing to fight for their country. Abigail had a reply to this ridiculous point. When it came to bravery, she would dryly remark, what man in battle had ever faced more danger or pain than a woman during the delivery of a child?

Once when a conceited young man remarked in public that he was quite willing to give women "all their rights *except* the right to vote" she inquired tartly, "Just how did our rights and privileges, political or otherwise, happen to come into your possession, my boy?"

Once when she was riding on a stagecoach in eastern Washington—the only woman among men, as she so often had to be—a fellow traveler who had been warming himself from time to time with a bottle he was carrying, decided to make Abigail the butt of some sarcastic remarks for the benefit of the other travelers. "Madame," he said, in ending these remarks, "you ought to be at home enjoying yourself like my wife is doing. I want to bear all the hardships of life myself, and let her sit by the fire, toasting her footsies."

Abigail had learned long since not to enter into arguments with drunks. She let the passengers poke their elbows into one another at her expense while she sat silent. But Abigail enjoyed an unexpected revenge when the man was dropped before his

house beside the road. There in the thickly falling snow stood his poor wife chopping away at the woodpile. Abigail couldn't resist this opportunity to make a point. She leaned out of the coach and called cheerfully to her tormentor, "Good-bye. I see that your wife is toasting her footsies." She could still laugh at that one when she was in her seventies.

The one thing Abigail could not endure was what she thought of as "pompous nonsense"—such a notion as, for instance, that by giving women the vote they would at once, in some mysterious way, become "coarse and masculine."

After her fame had spread across America she made a number of trips east. On one of these trips to attend a suffrage convention, she met the great Horace Greeley, editor of the New York *Tribune*. Greeley was then running for the Presidency of the United States. He received Abigail warmly because he had been told that she had made a speech in his favor. But when Abigail spoke of her mission—which was to ask him to endorse the Suffrage Movement in his political platform—he at once grew irritable. Stroking his much-caricatured white chin whiskers, he said in a voice suddenly "as hard as hailstones": "I don't want women to be men."

"Neither do I," replied Abigail, getting at once to her feet, preparing to leave with no more talk. "I wouldn't be a man if I could! And now, Mr. Greeley mark my words: you'll never be President! You will find that women can tear down, if they are not permitted to build up."

Her prophecy came true. Greeley never became President.

It was 1912 when Abigail Scott Duniway, by now an old woman in a lace cap, was at last able to sign the Equal Suffrage Proclamation for the state of Oregon. She had written the proclamation herself—an event said to be as significant in the long unrecorded history of women as the writing of the Constitution of the United States was to humanity in general. For no women had ever been entrusted with the framing of so important a paper.

Abigail Scott Duniway died three years later, in 1915. She had seen many changes in the status of women since the year 1876 when, as a keen-eyed visitor from the far West, she had made a special visit to the Women's Pavilion at the Philadelphia Centennial. There, to her distress, she had found no objects more significant than the dresses once worn by European royalty, or the baby caps of eminent American men. "Why not a faded calico dress and sunbonnet, a pair of homely shoes worn thin by tramping through the dust and stones of the American continent?" So Abigail, the pioneer, might well have wondered.

Right up to the day of her death, Abigail was reminding American women and girls of the gratitude they should feel for the hard fight that certain indomitable females had made in their behalf.

"The young women of today," she once said, "free to study, to speak, to write, to choose their occupations, should remember that every inch of this freedom was bought for them at a great price.

It is for them to show their gratitude by helping onward the reforms of their own times, by spreading the light of freedom and truth still wider."

And, finally, she voiced one great and simple challenge: "The debt that each generation owes to the past it must pay to the future."

Thus, Abigail, the pioneer path-breaker and prophet, pointed all American women on their way to an ever-widening world!

INDEX

LANDMARK BOOKS

WORLD LANDMARK BOOKS